China

Managing editor Chris Milsome
Editor Chester Fisher
Assistant Editor Dale Gunthorp
Design Patrick Frean
Picture Research Ed Harriman
Production Phillip Hughes
Illustrations John Shackell
Ron Hayward
John Mousdale
Marilyn Day
Sandra Archibald
Tony Payne
Tony Simmonds
Maps Matthews and Taylor Associates

Photographic sources Key to positions
of illustrations: (T) top, (C) centre,
(B) bottom, (L) left, (R) right

Associated Press: 49(BR), 53(BR) *Nick
Birch:* 27(BR) *British Museum:* 47(BL)

Camera Press: 20(BR), 37(TR), 44(BL),
45(TR), 45(BR) *Tim Canadine:* 2-3, 6-7,
8(T), 10(B), 11(T), 14-15, 16-17, 18-19,
22(BR), 23(TL), 26(T), 27(TR), 27(BL),
28-9, 30(CR), 30(B), 33(CR), 34(TR),
35(TL), 35(TR), 36(CL), 36(BR), 36(T),
37(CL), 41(BR), 43(BR), 49(BL), 50-51,
52(B) *Richard Clapp Photography:* 30(BL)
Mary Evans Picture Library: 39(TR) 38-39
(B), 47(TL) *Werner Forman Archive:* 10(B)
Granada Television: 12(B) *Richard and Sally
Greenhill:* 23(TR), 32(BL), 33(TR)
Gulbenkian Museum of Oriental Art: 13(TL),
26(TC) *Sonia Halliday Photographs:* 9(B),
46(B), 47(TR) *Robert Harding Associates:*
32(B), 34(B) *Michael Holford:* 26(B)
Keystone Press Agency: 43(BL) *Mansell
Collection:* 8(B), 39(BR), 40(CL), 40(BL)
Dennis Moore: 13(BR) *Radio Times Hulton
Picture Library:* 22(BL), 38(T), 40(BR),

41(BL), 42(TL), 46(TC) *Snark International:*
38(CB) *Society for Anglo-Chinese Under-
standing:* 12(T), 12(BL), 33(BR), 44(B),
45(TL), 50(B), 52(CL), 52(BL)
Productions Television Recontre: 41(TL),
41(TR), 47(BR) *Rex Features:* 43(TR),
48(T) *Roger Viollet:* 42(T)

First published 1974
Macdonald Educational Limited
Holywell House
London, E. C. 2

© Macdonald Educational
Limited 1974

ISBN 0 356 04852 7

Published in the United
States by Silver Burdett
Company, Morristown, N. J. .
1976 Printing

Library of Congress
Catalog Card No. 75-44869

China

the land and its people

Jonathan Hammond

Macdonald Educational

Contents

An ancient civilization

Classical China

The Chinese have a very ancient civilization, one of the oldest in the world. Cast bronze work of fine artistic quality was produced even before 2000 B.C., and the earliest known written records of about 1500 B.C. show that writing was already highly developed in those early times.

Since then, dynasties of rulers have come and gone. One of the earliest, the Chou, introduced the feudal system into China. Under this system all people had a place in a scale of authority and took orders from the group just above them. Feudalism had its uses at a time when banditry and lawlessness were rife, but in later years it became corrupt and oppressive.

The greatest feudal dynasties were the Han (206 B.C. to 220 A.D.), the T'ang (618–906 A.D.) and the Ming (1368–1644 A.D.) These produced able rulers who enriched the country through trade, and encouraged art, scholarship and philosophy.

The long decline

Chinese philosophy has two important features: it stresses logic, and the need for harmony in society. To achieve harmony, philosophers believed that those given power by the feudal system should be considerate, and those without power obedient. These ideas could be abused, and often were.

Chinese culture, for all its greatness, was available only to a very few, and those with power often forgot their philosophy. Greedy rulers impoverished their subjects, and so China fell into a long decline. In its weakened state it was an easy prey to European and Japanese empire-builders of the nineteenth century.

Today, China is on its feet again, and again the world is learning that people so rich in ideas and so determined to do everything well have much to contribute.

▲ The Human race has existed in China for 6,000,000 years. Peking Man lived in caves near Peking. These prehistoric people may have been the very remote ancestors of some modern Chinese.

The changing borders of China

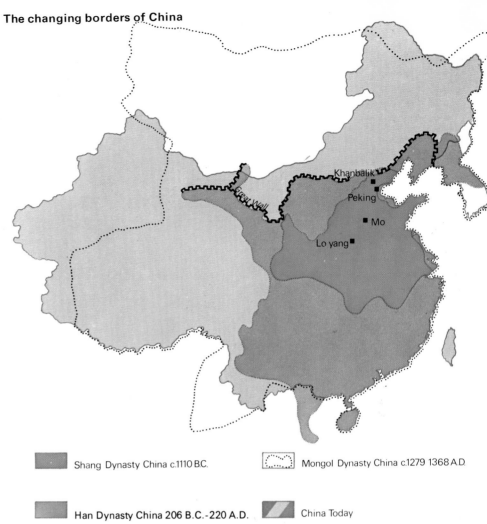

Khanbalik

Peking

Mo

Lo yang

Great Wall

▮	Shang Dynasty China c.1110 B.C.	⬚	Mongol Dynasty China c.1279 1368 A.D.
▮	Han Dynasty China 206 B.C.-220 A.D.	▨	China Today

▲ The periods of China's greatest growth were the Han dynasties, 206 B.C.–220 A.D., and Kublai Khan's reign (1279–1297).

Modern China evolved during the Manchu dynasty. It covers over ten million square kilometres.

▲ The Great Wall was built during the Han dynasties. It runs from the coast north of Peking across 3,000 kilometres (about 2,000 miles) of mountains and valleys, and ends in the north west. Han dynasty troops patrolled the wall to keep an eye on barbarian people from the north whose raids were a menace to the Han farmers.

◀ Genghis Khan, the most famous of the Chinese "warrior-emperors". His armies attacked the decaying Southern Sung dynasty early in the thirteenth century, using gunpowder and grenades. Under Kublai Khan the Mongol Empire, with its capital near Peking, extended westwards as far as the Black Sea.

▶ A Chinese engraving of 1811, showing courtiers in a procession led by the Manchu emperor. The emperor lived in the Forbidden City in the heart of Peking. He had almost no contact with the people, apart from high officials, courtiers and servants. Government by all-powerful, isolated emperors was to continue for another hundred years.

A vast and diverse land

The land

China is the third largest country in the world and covers over 10,000,000 square kilometres (almost 4,000,000 square miles). Some parts are harsh and inhospitable, others provide rich agricultural land. So most of China's 800,000,000 people live in a quarter of its area.

A third of the country is mountainous. Jolmo Lungma (Mount Everest) is the highest peak in the world. Some of China's deserts are among the world's cruellest. The Uighur word for the Taklamakan desert means "go in and you won't come out".

People in different areas grow quite different crops. Rice is the principal crop in the south. Further north, where frost prevents rice growing, wheat is cultivated.

Three great rivers cross China: the Huang Ho (or Yellow River), the Yangtse and the Sikiang. Along the lower reaches of these rivers there are fertile plains, but some are prone to flooding. The Huang Ho, was formerly called "China's sorrow", has taken millions of lives through floods, and has frequently changed its course. Since 1949 many new dams and dykes have been built to prove that "people are stronger than the river".

The people

Just as crops differ from one area to another, so do people's way of life and even racial features. The majority of the people (94 per cent) belong to the Han racial group. Foreigners think of Han people as *the* Chinese, but there are 50 nationalities, speaking many different languages. Many of these minority races live in the western half of China, some in the harsher and colder climates.

Tibet, the "roof of the world" is one minority region. It is a high plateau, cut off by the Himalayas on one side and the Kunlun mountains on the other. It is bitterly cold for most of the year. The Tibetans are a poor pastoral people, raising fleecy yaks which provide them with milk and wool. Recently better stock and some industry have been brought to Tibet. Human effort is slowly changing the face of China.

The many Han Chinese dialects

CHINA

ASIA

Han	Uighur
Tibetan	Kazakh
Mongol	Kirghiz

◀ In the north of China, the scenery is rugged. Ranges of high mountains like the Khangai in Inner Mongolia and the Altai and Tienshan in Sinkiang-Uigur abound. Parts of these mountain ranges are heavily cultivated.

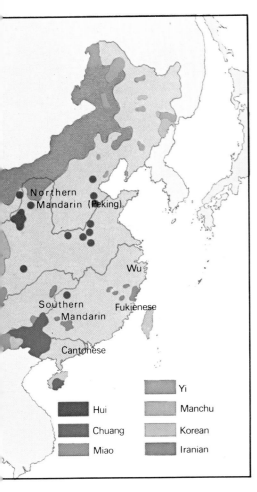

Northern
Mandarin (Peking)

Wu

Southern
Mandarin   Fukienese

Cantonese

	Hui		Yi
	Chuang		Manchu
	Miao		Korean
			Iranian

▼ Shanghai is China's biggest port and the city with the largest population in the world (over 10 million). Ships of many countries pass through its docks. Junks are the traditional Chinese craft for hauling goods.

▲ Agriculture is the foundation of the Chinese economy. One of the many reasons for the creation of communes in the 1950s was the need to increase food production. Some land, affected by soil erosion, needs treatment.

The different faces of China

▲ The Han are the majority people within China, 94 per cent of the population.

▲ About 4 million Uighur live in China, most in the Sinkiang-Uighur Autonomous Region.

▲ Of the 3½ million Tibetans over half live in other parts of China.

▲ 3½ million Chinese belong to the Yi nationality. They are scattered throughout China.

11

The Chinese influence

The oldest living civilization

China has the oldest continuing civilization in the world, and certainly one of the greatest. It is among the biggest countries in the world, and has more people than any other country. It has a social system quite unlike any known before. So China's influence on the world is bound to be very considerable.

All the East bears the imprint of Chinese culture, and many Eastern countries have, at various times, been part of Chinese empires. Japan and India, which have great civilizations of their own, have learned from China, given ideas or religions to China, and frequently warred with China.

Until the nineteenth century, Chinese influence on the West was restricted by distance, and by the mountains and deserts which fringe the land borders. Marco Polo visited China in the fourteenth century. He brought pasta back to Italy and vastly expanded trade, so that China became known to the West through its tea, silk and porcelain. Marco Polo brought back reports of many curious Chinese ways. He was surprised to notice that the Chinese made fire with a "black stone": coal was then unknown in Europe.

China today

Today the barriers of distance are down, and China has ended its policy of isolation. China's great political experiment is watched by the world with awe; in some places with admiration, in others with fear. Mao's brand of socialism is creating an entirely new kind of society. North Vietnam, Albania, Tanzania and Guinea are already attempting to build states modelled to some extent on China. Mao's socialism is based on an agricultural society, on the peasants. People are given intensive political, moral and technical training and are expected to turn their backs on luxury and personal enrichment so that the whole community may benefit from their efforts. So China today is the only country which has no motor cars owned for private pleasure, but many communally owned lorries which can carry farm produce as well as people.

China is a poor country, but a very different, very dynamic, very important one. It is already a world power. As a source of political and ethical ideas its influence may be even greater.

▲ The Chinese discovered silk weaving around 1,800 B.C. Trade in silk became important during the Han dynasties (206 B.C. to 220 A.D.) and still is today.

▶ The Tan-Zam railway connecting landlocked Zambia with the sea, is one of China's major foreign aid projects.

▼ Chinese experts demonstrating an anti-aircraft gun to North Vietnamese soldiers. The Chinese have given aid to the North Vietnamese during the long Vietnam war.

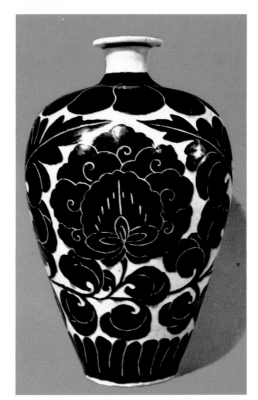

▲ This Mei-p'ing vase is an example of the beautiful ceramic work produced during the Sung dynasty (960–1279 A.D.).

▲ Chinese communism has influenced people far beyond the borders of China. Mao's *Little Red Book* is one of the classics of communist literature.

▲ China's trade has been an important link between East and West since the time of Marco Polo. Tea is especially important.

▲ A form of gunpowder for fireworks was used in China around 600 A.D., centuries before it was discovered in the West.

▲ Overseas Chinese live in six main areas —Taiwan, Hong Kong, Macao, the U.S.A., Britain and the Philippines.

▲ Chinese restaurants serving authentic Peking or Canton dishes are now prominent in nearly every Western country. The Lee Ho Fuk in Gerrard Street, London, is famous.

The family

Families old and new

In China traditions more than 2,000 years old are not unusual. Before the revolution the Chinese family was governed much as Confucius (551–479 B.C.), the greatest Chinese philosopher, had advised: the husband ruled the wife, the older children the younger children. Most wives work, and receive the same pay as men. Many children are better educated than their parents and have more responsibility in the family. Yet ancient traditions die hard, and the Chinese family is still dominated by fathers.

The government has undertaken an intensive campaign for birth control, but many couples still have five or six children. Housing is scarce and flats are small. Three generations often live together, so there is little space to spare and little privacy.

The Chou family

The Chous have four children. Chou Quo-chen and her husband are social workers, helping limbless people in a special hostel. They work eight hours a day and are paid 74 yuan (about £15) a month each. Mrs. Chou is also secretary of the branch of the Communist Party at the hostel, so she is a busy person.

In the evenings, she and her husband share the housework, and spend as much time as they can with the two younger children. The youngest is high-spirited and noisy, so Mrs. Chou worries about him. However, he is a cadre (class leader) at school, so she believes he has a more serious side to his nature. The third son is 16. He will soon do his army service and hopes, after that, to go to university.

The Chou family moved into their tiny house in 1952 and pay 10 yuan (about £2) a month in rent. They are satisfied with the life they lead and would be rather surprised to hear that many people in the West would call them poor.

▲ The hut resembling a dog-kennel was where two families lived before 1949. They now live in the modern block of flats.

▼ Old people usually live with their children and grandchildren. This grandmother looks after the child during the day.

A daily timetable for commune family

◀ Many houses in China are still very basic. These cottages on a poor commune, for instance, have no running water and no toilets. Electricity is supplied to the village hall, but not to individual houses. When the harvest has been gathered, these houses will have a face-lift before the cold weather comes. Outdoor living is the rule in summer.

▲ This family lives in a two-roomed flat in Shanghai. The two men are brothers. With them are the wife and daughter of one of them.

▼ The man in the family is becoming more involved in domestic duties. Before the revolution he would have regarded tea-making as beneath him.

8.00

8.30

12.00

2.00

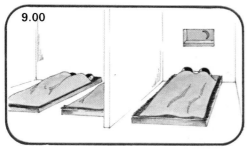

9.00

The essential commune

The layout of a typical commune diagram with labels:

- Administrative building
- Shop
- Playing field
- School
- Private plots

The layout of a typical commune

▲ The commune is often a group of villages with a central administration. It is organized with great care, for there are two aims it must achieve: it must be efficient, and it must give everyone the chance to take part in its running. The commune shown here is a small one. It has its central hall where meetings are held to discuss the farmwork, the commune's school, and to arrange cultural and leisure activities. People often gather at the hall in the evening to dance, act or play musical instruments.

Life in the commune

Eighty per cent of the Chinese people are peasants. The land belongs to them, not individually, but in groups known as communes. The diagram on this page shows a very small commune of four villages. Big or small they work in the same way: they have elected leaders who, with the help of government technicians, decide which crops to grow, and how to divide the work. They arrange housing, schooling and leisure activities for all the members.

Most communes grow several crops and, since the Cultural Revolution, communes have been trying to make most of the things they need. Even small communes have a blacksmith's shop, where they make ploughs and repair tractors.

Each family lives in a small single-storeyed house, usually made of clay or

▲ Workers spend on average about ten hours a day, six days a week, cultivating crops. The actual time varies according to the season. In winter there is much less work to do.

◄ Advanced communes grow food not only for their own inhabitants but also for the surrounding towns. The beans being packed in this picture are due to be sent to Tientsin.

16

stone. Each house has a private plot where the family grow fruit and vegetables or keep chickens.

China is the only poor Asian country to have put an end to famine. The commune system, which gave land to the peasants and taught them to use it productively, has made this possible.

Neighbourhood committees

In the towns it is not so easy for people to live and work communally, but they are able to manage their own local government through the system of neighbourhood committees. These groups run their own social services. They share out the streetcleaning duties, organize libraries, clinics for the sick, and take care of old people without families. They also run the schools, and arrange a tricycle service for kindergarten pupils.

▲ Prize litters of pigs are bred in the Sino-Korean People's Friendship Commune, seen here. Their bacon is eaten in Peking as well as on the commune.

◄ Rice is sifted and cleaned by workers before being eaten on the commune and before being sent out to shops in the towns. This long job gives people a chance to chat.

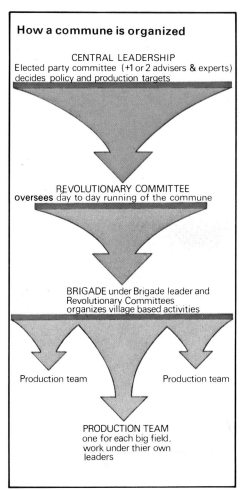

How a commune is organized

CENTRAL LEADERSHIP
Elected party committee (+1 or 2 advisers & experts) decides policy and production targets

REVOLUTIONARY COMMITTEE
oversees day to day running of the commune

BRIGADE under Brigade leader and Revolutionary Committees organizes village based activities

Production team   Production team

PRODUCTION TEAM
one for each big field, work under thier own leaders

Making the most of leisure

The cultural palaces

Chinese people spend one or two evenings a week at workers' cultural palaces run by the commune party committees or by neighbourhood committees in the towns. Here they play cards or Chinese chess, or they attend cultural courses. The subjects include painting, sculpture, pottery, learning to play musical instruments and singing; all the tutors are experts.

There are separate cultural palaces for children, open at weekends. The activities are much the same as at the workers' palaces, though the children prefer different subjects. Dancing, learning to shoot with air-rifles, making model aeroplanes and paintings are especially popular.

Time for development

The Chinese never think of their leisure as time to while away. All their views are heavily influenced by politics, and leisure is seen as time for development, both of mind and body. So many people get up at dawn to do calisthenics in the street. (Calisthenics are exercises designed to make the body stronger and more graceful.) Again there are experts to instruct, for the Chinese believe in doing everything well.

Sport is also taken seriously. Chinese teams are famous for their skill in table tennis. Basketball, volleyball and tennis are also played, and football, a newcomer to Chinese sport, is very popular.

▲ This photo was taken in a park in Tsinan. All parks are beautifully kept and are for the use and enjoyment of the people. Before the Revolution, they were mostly privately owned and only the owners and their friends could use them. As homes are very small, city dwellers make good use of these open spaces.

▲ Tsingtao in Shantung Province is one of the leading Chinese seaside resorts. It has many delightful sandy beaches. During the summer, people start work very early in the morning so that they can finish early and enjoy a leisurely afternoon.

► Cards are one of the favourite Chinese pastimes. Gambling was forbidden during the Cultural Revolution and cards were temporarily prohibited. But they have made a comeback since then, though they are no longer played for money. Interestingly enough, the cards have the same symbols as in the West—jack, queen, king.

▲ The Chinese are catching on to the ice-cream habit very fast. It has become very popular and is consumed in vast quantities during the summer. Sweets are also popular in China.

► Most public parks provide facilities for sport, including tennis. They also usually have a basketball or volleyball pitch. Badminton is another sport which the Chinese are beginning to take up.

▲ Basketball is one of the four most popular sports in China. It forms part of the curriculum of all middle schools.

► In most towns and cities, children aged between 5 and 17 go at weekends to children's cultural palaces, where, among other things, they play musical instruments.

Eating the Chinese way

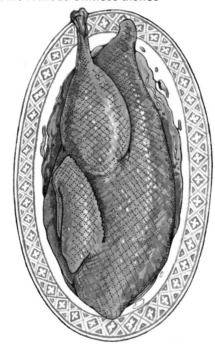

Everyday eating

The staple diet for many Chinese people is rice. Before the 1949 Revolution, many people were hungry all their lives, and malnutrition caused serious diseases. Now, everyone has enough to eat. More luxurious foods include chicken, sweet and sour pork, bamboo shoots, bean curd, vegetables of various descriptions and fish and other seafood (including sea-slugs). Soups of various kinds are also popular. Chinese desserts are usually simple fruits like lychees, mangoes and melons.

Most Chinese people eat three meals each day. Weekday meals are usually simple, made from the produce of the commune and the family's vegetable garden. The village shops provide more exotic fare for special occasions. The Chinese drink large quantities of tea. They are also fond of beer and, for special occasions, rice wine.

Chinese food is always prepared in bite-sized pieces, and knives never appear on the table. In China, knives belong to the kitchen, and people use chopsticks or spoons as eating utensils. Traditional Chinese cooking is imaginative, wholesome and tasty. Food is quickly cooked, so retains most of its vitamins and, even from a few simple ingredients, a Chinese cook can make varied and attractive dishes.

Banquets

Foreign visitors are always lavishly treated to the best of China's food. At dinners and banquets guests are offered a variety of dishes, so that they can choose their own favourites. Chinese cooking is famous and in many countries Chinese restaurants draw people who like to eat well. Chinese restaurants in China are often less luxurious, but the food is just as good.

▲ This dish is one of the main Chinese delicacies. The ducks are bred on a special farm just outside of Peking. The meal is generally served at state banquets and special occasions, surrounded by bean curd and vegetables of all descriptions. It is cooked to a special temperature and is really delicious.

▲ Fish and black olives served in sweet and sour sauce, from Canton. The regions of China differ widely in their cuisine. Most Chinese restaurants in the West serve Cantonese food. Peking food is considered to be the most delicate in flavour and many restaurants specialise in it.

▲ Families living in communes sometimes eat picnic meals in the fields. Meals at home are also simple, made of vegetables from the family's plot and rice, wheat or millet.

A typical day's meals in a commune

Breakfast
Millet porridge, maize bread and a vegetable dish of tomatoes, beans and potatoes fried in oil. Water or tea.

Lunch
Steamed golden rice, vegetable dish as for breakfast, soup of vegetable water. Fried chillies. Tea.

Supper
Millet porridge.

How to use chopsticks

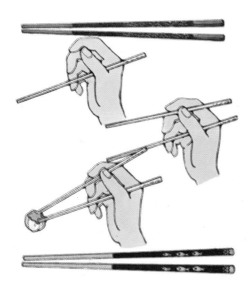

▲ Take one stick between the thumb and first two fingers. The other rests against the third finger. Only the upper chopstick is moved. After a little practice, eating is quite easy.

Make yourself a Chinese meal

You may have to visit a Chinese shop to collect all the ingredients for this meal. The best method is to prepare all the dishes in advance, then cook them a few minutes before serving.

SWEET AND SOUR PORK
1 lb pork
1 beaten egg
oil for deep drying
(ingredients for the sauce)
1 green pepper, chopped
1 small onion, chopped
2 tablespoons vinegar
4 teaspoons sugar
2 teaspoons tomato sauce
2 teaspoons cornflour
2 teaspoons soy sauce
$\frac{1}{2}$ pint cold water

Cut the pork into 1-inch cubes and sprinkle with salt. Dip cubes into egg, then into cornflour. Fry in hot oil till golden brown. Lift out the cubes.
Lightly fry the onion and green pepper. Mix all the other ingredients for the sauce in a cup, then add to the onion and green pepper. Simmer gently for five minutes. Pour the sauce over the pork pieces and serve.

BEAN CURD
(This dish may be left out if bean curd is difficult to find in your local shops.) Cut the bean curd into cubes. Deep fry for one minute in the oil used for the pork. Drain and serve.

NOODLE AND MEAT BALL SOUP
$\frac{1}{4}$ lb minced beef
$\frac{1}{2}$ egg
$\frac{1}{2}$ cup soft noodles
vegetable stock, or a stock cube
2 teaspoons cornflour

Mix the minced beef with the egg, salt and pepper, roll into small balls and fry lightly for five minutes. Heat the vegetable stock (or melted stock cube) in a pan. Add water to make 5 cups of liquid. Mix the cornflour with a little cold water in a cup, and pour it into the stock. Boil, stirring constantly. Then add salt, meatballs and noodles, and simmer gently for ten minutes.

FRIED MIXED VEGETABLES
$\frac{1}{4}$ lb mushrooms
2 oz bamboo shoots
1 small cucumber
1 small carrot
1 onion
1 stick celery
1 cup bean sprouts
3 tablespoons oil
$\frac{1}{2}$ teaspoon sugar
1 tablespoon soy sauce
$\frac{1}{2}$ cup cold water
2 teaspoons cornflour

Wash the vegetables. Cut them into slices (except the bean sprouts). Heat the oil and fry all the vegetables gently for two minutes. Mix the other ingredients in a cup, then add to the vegetables and boil, stirring all the time, for one minute. Serve.

FRIED RICE WITH EGG
3 cups cooked cold rice
2 spring onions, chopped
2 tablespoons cooked green peas
$1\frac{1}{2}$ eggs, beaten (use the $\frac{1}{2}$ egg left over from the soup)

Mix the beaten eggs with the spring onion and fry in a little oil till the eggs have set. Turn the heat to low. Stir in the other ingredients, mix well till the mixture is heated.

The pork, bean curd, mixed vegetables and rice, each on its own dish, should be served at the same time. Put China tea on the table, and let your guests help themselves. Let them try chopsticks.

Education for a new society

The examination system

Educated people have always been highly respected in China. In the third century B.C. the emperor introduced a system of examinations for the civil service. These papers tested an applicant's knowledge of the Confucian classics, for the rulers believed that people who understood Confucius would be more honest and able administrators. At its best, the system produced fearless administrators who defended peasants against powerful barons.

The system was intended to be democratic, but Chinese education was very severe; it takes years of concentrated study to master the script, and all education had to be paid for. By 1949 China had a small group of very highly educated people, while the vast majority had no education at all.

Schools of the revolution

Today the Chinese script has been somewhat simplified, schooling is free to families who cannot afford the low fees. Many of the schools have been built by the commune members themselves. The buildings are plain, and books and equipment scarce, but people take great pride in their own schools and their achievements.

Children attend primary school from the ages of seven to twelve. Language study takes half the school day; other subjects are politics, mathematics, painting, physical education and singing. Pupils in the more senior grades spend ten days a year working in the fields, learning about agriculture.

The next step is middle school, which pupils attend from 12 to 17. Here they study subjects like those taught in Western countries, though the emphasis is different. All subjects are closely related to politics. Another difference is that pupils spend two months of each year working in factories or in school workshops. The Chinese believe that the best way to learn how things are made is to make them oneself, and to work with the people whose skills have grown from years of experience.

Before going to university, students have to spend two years working in a factory, on a commune, or in the army. All students study the works of Marx, Lenin, Mao and other socialist philosophers. Student grants are very small. The students are expected to lead Spartan lives and always to remember that the community has given them education so that they may serve all the people.

Education is a serious matter in China.

▲ Confucius, or Kung Fu-tzu (meaning "Kung the teacher") lived from 551 to 479 B.C. He believed that people should live according to a strict moral order. His teachings, which stressed self-discipline and respect for ancient learning, were the basis of Chinese education until 1967.

▶ Middle school students learn many different subjects. The school day lasts for eight hours and consists partly of academic lessons and partly of practical work in workshops and factories.

▲ Physical training and gymnastics are part of every primary and middle school's day.

▶ At special Cadre schools leaders among the workers study Marxism and work the fields.

The Chinese system of education

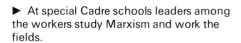

Kindergarten 2-7

Primary school 7-12 .

Junior middle school 12-15

Senior middle school 15-17

Work in commune, factory or army 17-19

University 19-22

Heroes of the people

▲ A scene from the famous story, *Pilgrimage to the West,* written in 1119 A.D. The novel recounts the adventures of a monk Huan Tsang who is sent to India to find sacred writings. One of his companions on the journey is Monkey, king of the monkeys, who is trying to become a saint. Monkey has many fantastic adventures on the way. He is able to fly and to change into different shapes. Because Monkey is frequently mischievous, he is made to wear a tight iron helmet to control his actions. Monkey wears the helmet so long that when he is allowed to take it off he has forgotten that he had it on.

▶ The most famous Chinese novel is *The Dream of the Red Chamber* which appeared about 1765. It tells of the rise and decline of the Chia family, who were very powerful. The hero and heroines are young people and the novel deals with their desire for freedom and happiness. However the older people insist that they follow the rules laid by tradition. Generations of Chinese boys and girls have identified themselves with characters in the book. The book was the first that dared to describe real people and situations. It was much criticized for having a bad influence on the young.

Heroes of courage and foresight

The heroes of the Chinese are usually people who have set a political or moral example by their actions. Most of the heroes of feudal times were people of special valour.

Chen Ho, for instance, was a great navigator of the fifteenth century. He made seven voyages to the islands of the South China Seas and to the coasts of India, Arabia and East Africa. Three of his fleets carried 27,000 men each. These explorations vastly expanded China's trade.

Chan Tien-yu, China's first railway engineer, constructed the Peking-Inner Mongolia railway in 1905, the first to be built in China under Chinese direction.

During feudal times, many stories were told about groups of outlaws who fought cruel landlords, and gave much of their booty to poor peasants. These stories were banned during the Manchu period, but have now been revived. China's Robin Hoods are numerous, and their courage, skill in fighting, and the tricks they played on wicked landlords make them great favourites.

New heroes also abound. The Chinese admire the grand and heroic, so many ordinary people who do especially brave or unselfish things earn a place in legend.

◄ The Chinese today admire courage and self-sacrifice especially when in the service of the people. This scene shows Young Peng attempting to put out a forest fire. He is a real "barefoot" doctor who was collecting herbs in the mountains when a thunderstorm broke out. Lightning set fire to the forest and was threatening to engulf houses in a village. The villagers tried to stop the fire and Young Peng helped with medical aid. He then seized a club and went into the heart of the fire. After he injured his foot, his hair caught fire, and he toppled into the flames. He was rescued just in time. His courage has been held up as an example to all young people.

▼ An illustration taken from a children's picture story in the magazine *China Pictorial*. The story tells of two children on a fishing expedition and the curious adventures they have, encountering whirlpools and huge fish. Many such stories of adventure are published for children in China.

▲ Norman Bethune was a Canadian doctor who went to China in 1938 to help Mao's armies in the field. Mao Tse-tung was so impressed by his devotion and hard work that he made him a symbol of international friendship to the Chinese cause. In 1939, after nearly two years' work in China, Bethune contracted blood poisoning while operating on wounded soldiers, and died.

（14）姐弟俩跟踪大鲟鱼来到水深浪激的湖中心。鲟鱼被几十个挂钩挂痛了，在水中拚命挣扎，掀起了一个个大漩涡，使小船在浪涛中猛烈颠簸。

Arts old and new

Theatre and the Cultural Revolution

The Chinese artistic tradition is 3,000 years old. In painting, music, literature and ceramics China has developed styles quite different from Western art. However, since the eighteenth century Western art has been influenced by Chinese works, and until recently some Chinese arts were influenced by the "social realist" artists of Russia.

Artists in classical times tried to reach perfection as defined by Confucius: work should be harmonious, beautiful, and raise the imagination out of everyday life. The painting on this page is characteristic of work in the classical style, though paintings of beautiful landscapes are more common.

Today much has changed, but the view that art helps to make people better remains. There has been a move in painting towards more realistic work, often depicting great heroes and scenes from the revolutions. New Chinese literature and poetry are more political, and always have a moral. Art today is intended to be for all the people.

In the theatre the old comedies about princes, nobles and courtesans have been replaced by tales about heroic peasants who save a village from disaster, or courageous workers opposing Japanese invaders. These stories are fitted into a traditional Chinese form called Peking opera. Ballet, acrobatics, singing and spectacular scenery are mixed with the story into a colourful whole.

The Russian influence

The Russians introduced ballet into China after 1949. In a short time, amateur and professional groups were performing full-scale Russian ballets, like *Swan Lake*, before enthusiastic crowds. Russian ballets have been abolished since the Cultural Revolution, though the techniques remain. The most popular ballets are *The White-Haired Girl* and *The Red Detachment of Women*. Both tell stories about the revolution, and both are designed to appeal to everybody.

▲ Soapstone figure of the Taoist god of long life, carved during the Ch'ing dynasty (eighteenth century).

▼ *Game of Polo* is probably based on an original by Li-Lin (1280–1368).

▲ Peking Opera is an old artistic form now given a revolutionary content. *Feng Lin Ao* describes the civil war in the 1920s.

▲ In traditional Chinese architecture proportions are carefully worked out to produce buildings with graceful lines.

▼ Many small workshops in neighbourhood committees produce traditional Chinese silk paintings.

▲ A boy playing the Chinese violin. The Chinese have a rich musical heritage. They have written scores dating from the seventh century A.D., and the music of ancient shepherds is still played on the *chin*, a seven-stringed lute. Flutes, gongs, drums and stringed instruments, related to this violin, are used in traditional music, which has been emphasized since the Cultural Revolution.

The birth of Chinese industry

The recovery of Chinese industry

Chinese industry was almost destroyed in the first half of this century. Cheap mass-produced cotton and plastic goods from Japanese or European factories had driven Chinese craftsmen to ruin, and native industries had not the money to buy modern equipment. Today China has its own industries, from basic steelworks which make machines for other factories, to the finest precision instruments used by surgeons. Traditional industries, like carpet weaving, silk printing, and food canning are also flourishing. Less than a quarter of the population work in industry, yet they produce three-quarters of the nation's wealth.

Educating the workers

Every factory provides education for its workers. This includes training about the industry, reading and writing lessons for those who need them, and political instruction. Also, instead of competing, factories learn from each other and any new methods or processes are shared.

Small factories, called collectives, are owned by their workers. Many of these are part of communes. Larger factories are owned by the state. The state factories are very important to the economy of China, and their workers receive higher pay.

China now produces its own lorries, tractors and cars. Their design has changed very little since the Russians withdrew, so they look old fashioned to Western people. The Chinese would reply that instead of bringing out new models every year, they keep parts as simple and standard as possible. So spares are cheaper, and it is easier for people to be their own mechanics.

▲ After the Cultural Revolution, many steel furnaces were set up in back yards and communes. Though many people thought them too small to be efficient, they have helped to make the communes more independent.

◄ The bulk of Chinese heavy industry is in the north-east. These steelworks are in Anshan. Railway lines are being made.

▲ Textiles are manufactured mostly in Shantung Province. This factory is in Tsingtao.

Some products of light industry

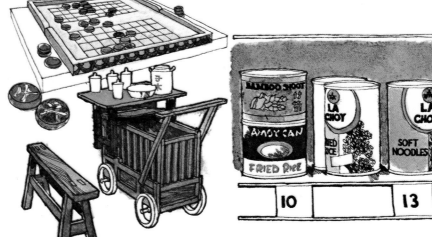

▲ Timber goods made for the home market are sturdily built and simple in design.

▲ Chinese tinned foods are of good quality, and sell well in overseas markets.

▲ This bridge, 2.5 kilometres long, is in two tiers, road on top, rail underneath. It was built over the River Yangtse from 1960—8. Originally it was planned by Russian advisers who backed out after the Sino-Soviet split in 1960. It was eventually completed by the Chinese, and is a great feat of engineering.

▲ Millions of bicycles are made in China, where they are a vital means of transport.

▲ Chinese cottons are printed in many patterns, or dyed in strong plain colours.

▲ This carpet factory near Tientsin makes carpets in traditional designs for export.

▶ Especially good workers are honoured. In this factory in Shenyang pictures of the model workers have been pinned on the wall.

29

The vital role of communication

Spreading the message

Chinese socialism relies on millions of individual people working towards the same goal: building a stronger, more revolutionary China. Information about new achievements, pep-talks and political instruction are essential to keep people enthusiastic, so a vast communications network has developed.

Newspapers, magazines, radio and television are all part of the network. There are also many huge posters, and leaders travel round the country speaking to groups of peasants and workers.

Much depends on people being able to read the complicated Chinese script. The great spread of education has brought literacy to most young people, but many of the older generation still gather in groups to hear a "party reader" read items of special interest from the newspapers.

The *Peking Daily* and the *People's Daily* are the main national papers. There are also local papers. The *Tsingtao Daily* is one. It has only four pages, yet covers local, national and world news, industry, agriculture, sport and culture. There are no advertisements.

Wall newspapers

Posters and "wall newspapers" are found all over China. Pictures of important socialist philosophers—Marx, Lenin and Mao—line the streets, sometimes dwarfing the cyclists and market stalls. Many people paint quotations from the thoughts of Mao on their houses and, since not everyone can buy a newspaper, items of special interest are often written out on big sheets of paper and pasted up in public places.

Foreigners may think that the Chinese tolerate rather a lot of sermonizing. The Chinese would reply that Western people are also bombarded with messages, but messages to "buy this" or "eat that", and that Chinese media do help to make all the people feel involved in China's progress.

▲ "Wall newspapers" are a cheap means of communication. They relate special items of news, or sometimes quote the words of national leaders. These "newspapers" will be read by workers passing the Shanghai docks on their way home.

▼ The main Chinese national newspapers are the *Peking Daily* and the *People's Daily*. The *People's Daily* is the organ of the Chinese Communist Party. Magazines include *Peking Review*, a theoretical journal, *China Reconstructs* and *China Pictorial*.

How Chinese is written

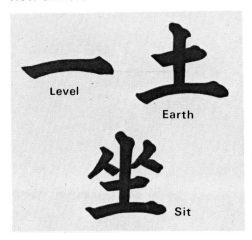

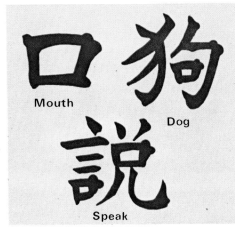

Level

Earth

Sit

Mouth

Dog

Speak

Friend   China (Centre Country)

Thief

▲ The first of these characters means "level". The second character, "earth", shows a tree on "the level". "Sit" shows a person on "the level".

▲ Characters grow out of each other. "Dog" has a great mouth in the middle, and so has "speak". The simple character "mouth" appears in many words.

▲ Characters can grow into very complex forms. The character for "friend" puts two "person" characters close together, while "thief" shows quite a different relationship!

抗日根据地军民遵照毛主席的教导，坚持自力更生，艰苦奋斗的方针，开展大生产运动，克服了严重的经济困难，为抗日战争的胜利奠定了物质基础。这是八路军战士在打场。

Following Chairman Mao's principle of self-reliance and hard struggle, the armed forces and people in the anti-Japanese base areas launched an extensive production campaign to overcome the severe material difficulties and thus laid the material foundations for victory in the anti-Japanese war. Photo shows fighters of the Eighth Route Army working on a thrashing ground.

▲ Chinese typewriters have a complex keyboard. There are 2,000 basic characters in the Chinese script, though a highly literate person will know three times as many!

▲ The ancient Chinese wrote by cutting characters into pieces of bamboo. After the third century A.D., when ink and paper were invented, writing became a highly-skilled craft. Characters were painted with brush pens, and beautifully formed writing was much admired. This art of calligraphy ranks with painting in China. Today mass education and the ball-point pen have undermined calligraphy, and fewer people are learning to use brush pens.

▶ Posters are mostly used in China for political purposes. They exhort the Chinese to produce more, to contribute more to humanity, or to heed some saying of Mao or Lenin. They are boldly designed, both in their pictures and their calligraphy.

The People's Liberation Army

▲ Where a factory or commune is backward —or simply short of workers—soldiers are often sent to help out, as shown here where soldiers are making bean curd.

▼ Ideological training has always been a prominent feature of the P.L.A. following Mao's dictum that the Party must control the gun, never the reverse.

The Fourth Red Army

The People's Liberation Army is the national army of China. The members wear green uniforms and matching caps. There are no badges of office, so a general and a soldier from the ranks dress alike. P.L.A. cadres also work in factories and on the land, for they are expected to know how to plough as well as how to shoot. Young people often do two years' army service before going to university.

The P.L.A. began as a revolutionary band of guerrilla fighters in 1927 led by Mao Tse-tung and Chu Teh and called the Fourth Red Army. Chiang Kai-shek, then leader of the government, sent troops against the communists. This was the beginning of the long civil war. At that time peasants were suffering from greedy landlords, and many joined Mao's forces. They were given training in Mao's guerrilla tactics:

When the enemy advances, we retreat.
When he escapes, we harass.
When he retreats, we pursue.
When he is tired, we attack.

The Long March

In 1934 Chiang launched a full-scale attack in an attempt to rout out the "bandits". The guerrillas, encircled and attacked from all sides, were forced to retreat to a communist stronghold on China's north-west border. On this Long March, 100,000 soldiers covered 5,000 miles. They crossed 18 mountain ranges, battled with Chiang's troops and the private armies of ten warlords —all in one year. Only 20,000 reached Yenan. From these toughened fighters the P.L.A. grew in numbers and power, for they had won support along the route and had exhausted Chiang's large forces.

How the Army is organized

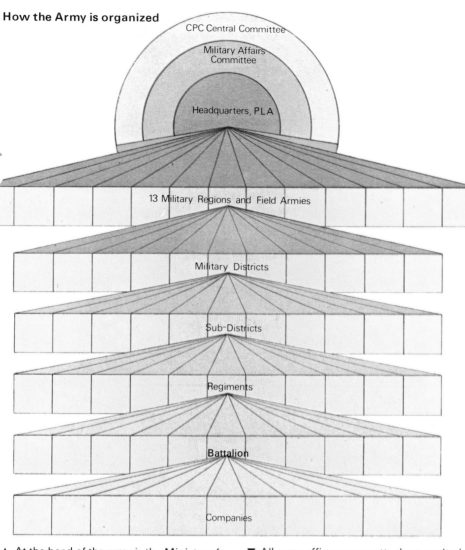

CPC Central Committee

Military Affairs Committee

Headquarters, PLA

13 Military Regions and Field Armies

Military Districts

Sub-Districts

Regiments

Battalion

Companies

▲ Where labour is scarce, P.L.A. members are drafted in to help. This telegraph operator works at the railway station in Erlian, a town on the Chinese-Mongolian border.

▲ At the head of the army is the Minister of Defence. Immediately under him is the Army Party Committee. The army is subdivided into 13 regional commands. Each of these has its own Party committee and consists of battalions and companies.

▼ All army officers, no matter how exalted, have to do manual labour each month, so as not to develop a "superior" outlook. These three men, sent to help out in a rice-growing area, are generals. They wear no badges of rank.

▼ Russia helped China to establish its socialist system, but the friendship between the two countries ended abruptly in 1960. Now the Sino-Soviet split has widened, and Chinese troops patrol the border with Russia, on the watch for hostilities.

Peking
heart of China

▶ There are about five million bicycles in Peking. Bicycles are the commonest form of transport; they cost nothing to run, are easy to park, and provide fresh air and exercise. There are few motor vehicles on the streets, so cycling is not dangerous. Here a traffic policeman directs cyclists and pedestrians. The portraits of Karl Marx and Frederick Engels on the hoardings remind bypassers of the early philosophers of socialism.

The ancient capital

Peking has been the capital of China since ancient times, with a single break from 1928–49. It is built on a traditional pattern, a series of rectangles enclosed by walls. The Imperial Palace was in the middle of the rectangles. In the inmost sanctuary of the Forbidden City (no longer forbidden to anyone) are the golden-roofed palaces, courtyards and gardens from which successive Emperors held sway over China.

Also in Peking are the Summer Palace, where Emperors and the court spent holidays in the warm weather, and the Temple of Heaven, where the Emperor made ritual sacrifices every spring to ensure a good harvest.

Peking today

In Peking today the present and the past merge together harmoniously. The population is huge, 7.8 million, yet the overall atmosphere is very relaxed, quite unlike hectic Western cities. Few private cars clog up the roads and, though there is an efficient bus service, most people get around on bicycles.

In the centre of Peking is Tien An Minh Square, containing the Great Hall of the People. On many buildings are huge bill-

▲ Prices are low in Peking. Shops, markets and individual stalls like the one shown here sell all kinds of domestic goods. This little stall is mounted on bicycle wheels, and the stall-keeper will pile up her stock and stool, and wheel them home in the evening, after the last customer has finished shopping.

▶ Tien An Minh square, main entrance to the Old Imperial City. Tien An Minh means "Gate of Heavenly Peace". In this square, Mao proclaimed the People's Republic of China in 1949. Important public announcements are still made in the square, and many public meetings are held here.

boards of Marx, Engels, Lenin, Stalin, and, with pride of place, Mao.

New buildings are also going up at great speed: schools, blocks of flats, multi-storeyed hotels and conference centres.

Peking has many museums and libraries. Since the revolution, old and interesting books and works of art have disappeared from the "junk" shops. They have been bought by the government for libraries and museums. Museums of history, Chinese art, revolution, geology, astronomy, natural history, humankind and many others have become rich storehouses of history and knowledge. They are always crowded, but guides (all women) keep order and provide explanations.

Many tiny, amazingly cheap restaurants serving excellent food and wine are found all over the city. Some are just a few tables in the corner of a shop, others specialize in the food of different regions. Saturday evening is the most popular time for family visits.

Peking has scores of shops and stores. Street traders jostle along the side streets selling guavas and mangoes. One back street has a maze of antique shops, selling jade figurines, chessboards and traditional pictures and designs of various kinds.

Things to see in Peking

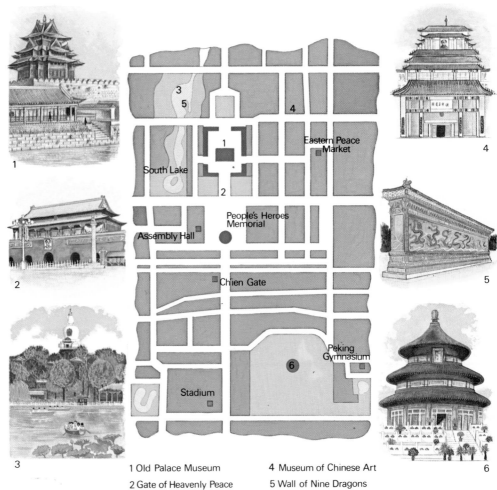

1 Old Palace Museum
2 Gate of Heavenly Peace
3 North Lake Park
4 Museum of Chinese Art
5 Wall of Nine Dragons
6 Altar of Heaven

▼ The suburbs of Peking stretch for miles. Most people live in single-storey houses, and many trees are visible over the line of low roofs. The families in this street have two or three roomed apartments. They spend much of their leisure time at cultural palaces, museums, libraries, or the ever-popular parks.

New approaches to medicine

Ancient and modern

Traditional Chinese medicines have been revived in China. These include herbal remedies and acupuncture. Acupuncture is a system of inserting needles into different parts of the body, then turning or agitating them gently, to stimulate "nerves" connected with diseased areas. Nobody quite understands why it works, but acupuncture has been found effective in the treatment of bronchitis, rheumatism, migraine headaches, and many other ailments. It is also used as a local anaesthetic for operations.

Before 1967 the traditional medicine was regarded as old-fashioned and primitive by qualified doctors. The Cultural Revolution brought a new interest to many traditions and to peasant culture, so the old medicine became respectable and now both sorts of medicine are practised. Herbal remedies save on expensive drugs, and for some diseases they seem to be more effective.

The sick country

In 1949 China was literally a sick country. Venereal disease and schistosomiasis (snail's disease) between them afflicted nearly a quarter of the population. The diseases which follow on famine and malnutrition were also rife, and there were very few doctors. Now all medical treatment is free, and life expectancy has increased from 28–35 years to 55–60 years.

The "barefoot doctors"

"Barefoot doctors" have emerged since the Cultural Revolution. They are ordinary workers and peasants trained to deal with common ailments. They treat simple injuries and infections and teach their comrades to understand hygiene. They also free physicians and surgeons for serious illnesses.

Acupuncture in action

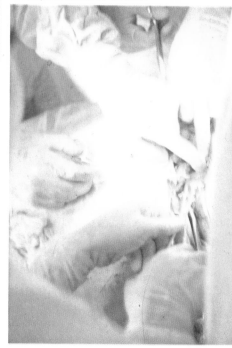

▲ This man is having a throat tumour removed under acupuncture used as a local anaesthetic. He is fully conscious and watches the operation being performed on himself with interest. Acupuncture is a remarkable folk medicine which is used in combination with modern treatments on a whole series of operations, serious and minor. The Chinese are at present engaged in research to find out why it works.

▶ The same man after the operation, his throat stitched up, none the worse for his ordeal. The decision to use acupuncture in his case was probably taken after discussions between the doctor, surgeon and patient, as well as his family and the revolutionary committee of his workplace.

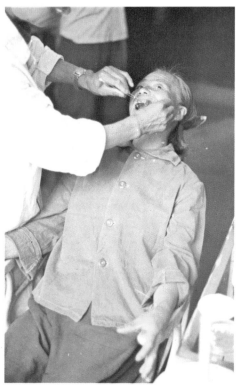

▲ This woman is having a tooth removed under local acupuncture anaesthesia. Dental treatment has improved enormously since the 1949 Revolution. Like doctors, dentists use a mixture of traditional and Western techniques and treatments.

▶ Most neighbourhood committees and factories have their own clinics and dispensaries, where minor ailments and hurts can be treated. Many of the workers take turns as volunteer nurses. This helps relieve the shortage of medical staff, and in this way many people learn more about medicine and health.

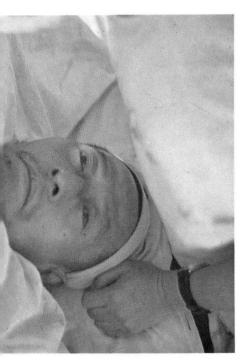

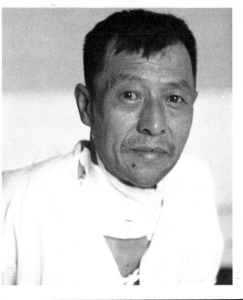

Acupuncture—the Chinese science

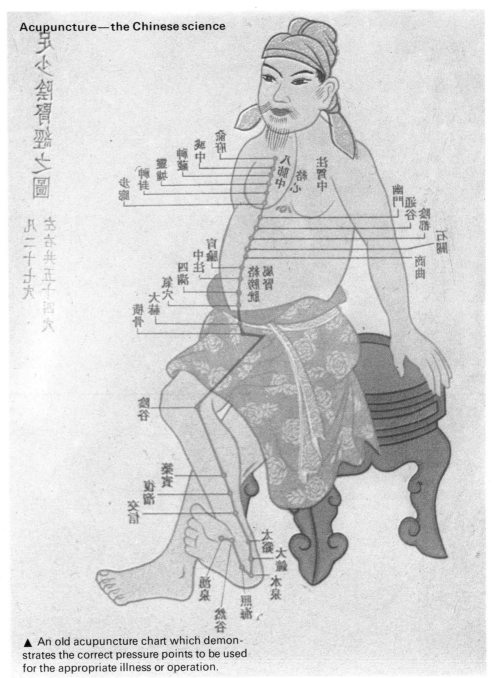

▲ An old acupuncture chart which demonstrates the correct pressure points to be used for the appropriate illness or operation.

► Herbs of various kinds have been used in the folk remedies of many countries. For centuries the Chinese peasants had no other medicine and, through accidental discovery and trial and error, medical folklore evolved. Later, Western "wonder drugs" (particularly antibiotics) were introduced, and the old remedies were gradually discarded. Then, in 1958, Chairman Mao instructed medical scientists to study the traditional medicines. Scientific investigation revealed that certain common herbs do have healing qualities. Some, like varieties of mint, help relieve headaches. Others, like cannabis used with discretion, can relieve mental stress and stomach troubles caused by tension. "Barefoot doctors" skilled in herbalism, now work among the villagers.

Taraxacum Officinale (A variety of dandelion)

Stomach and digestion

Acorus Calamus (Sweet Flag)

Heart, circulation, antiseptic

Mentha Arvensis (A variety of mint)

Pain-killer, restorative

The imperial twilight

Three centuries of Manchu rule

The Ching or Manchu dynasty lasted from 1644 to 1911. Its early history was illustrious. At its height, it ruled not only over the whole of present-day China but also received tribute from Nepal, Burma, Laos, Thailand, Annam, the Liu Ch'iu Islands and Korea. Its two outstanding personalities were the Emperors Kang H'si (1661–1722) and Ch'ien Lung (1736–1796).

Kang H'si had great physical energy, and an active and inquiring mind. He expanded China's frontiers and gave it a vigorous administration. Ch'ien Lung was also an extremely able ruler. He expanded China's frontiers even further than his predecessor.

The long decline

After Ch'ien, the Manchus went into a steady decline. European traders had discovered that China was a country of fine products and weak rulers. They set about buying and selling without reference to the government. British traders simply refused to obey imperial regulations and smuggled large quantities of opium into China. Drug addiction became a scourge, and the emperor declared war on Britain in an attempt to put a stop to the dealing. Britain won the war, so opium selling continued, and the British gained Hong Kong as well. French, American, Japanese, Russian and German traders followed.

For a while, the decline was halted by the Dowager Empress Tzu Hsi, or "Old Buddha". She dominated a succession of feeble rulers. Though she prevented any reforms, she at least held China together at a time when it was reeling under the impact of the West.

The Manchu dynasty ended in disaster. In 1894–5 China was crushingly defeated by Japan. As a result the trading nations claimed land, railways, and further buying and selling rights. China was virtually split up into colonies. Chinese patriots developed a great hatred of foreigners, and the Boxer Rebellion of 1898 was one attempt to drive them out.

Dr. Sun Yat-sen's call for a free, united, Republican China put an end to the Manchu dynasty 13 years later.

▲ This cartoon, published by *La Silhouette* in Paris, 1898, satirizes various foreign countries, greedily carving up China.

▼ Large numbers of Chinese became addicted to opium after the two Opium Wars and most towns and cities had their dope rings.

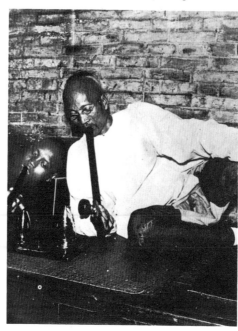

Foreign influences in China to 1912

INNER MONGOLIA

Port Arthur
Weihaiwei
Tsingtao
Korean Peninsula
Soochow
Hangchow
CHINA
Foochow
Kwangchowwan
Kowloon
Macao
Hong Kong
TAIWAN

Japan
British
Germany
Portugal
France
Extent of the Boxer Rebellion

▲ China was defeated by Japan in 1894. This began a rush by Western nations to gain small pieces of territory from which they could expand their economic control.

▼ During the First Opium War (1839–42), the East India Company's steamer *Nemesis* and the boats of the *Sulphur* and other ships destroyed the Chinese war junks in Anson's Bay, on January 7, 1841.

▲ The Boxer Rebellion (1898) was an uprising of peasants against foreign domination in China. It was crushed.

▼ The Empress Dowager Tzu Hsi was the real ruler of China during the late Manchu years. She suppressed all attempts at reform, but at least kept China from disintegrating.

Sun Yat-sen prophet of revolution

▲ Sun first went to school in Hawaii, and he later studied medicine at hospitals in Hong Kong and Canton. He did not turn seriously to politics until 1894, when the humiliating defeat of China by Japan turned him against the Manchus.

The professional revolutionary

Sun Yat-sen was China's first professional revolutionary, and Republican China's first president. He was born in South China in November 1866. Sun was convinced that China would never recover from its dreadful decline until the Manchu dynasty had been overthrown and replaced by a republic. He was a zealous and energetic person, and travelled widely, talking to large and small groups, organizing revolutionaries, raising money to buy arms. The cause seemed hopeless at times, but Sun's efforts never flagged. His first defeat occurred in 1895 when, just as the revolutionaries were about to strike, the authorities discovered their cache of 500 revolvers, and executed one of Sun's friends. By 1911 Sun had been defeated in ten attempts to overthrow the regime. The Chinese people, poor, hungry and without hope, seemed too depressed to rise.

President Sun

Suddenly things changed. In September 1911, after a revolt at Wuchang, the revolution suddenly took fire and the Manchus toppled. The emperor fled and a republic was declared in Peking with Sun as its provisional president. There was rejoicing in

▼ Before the 1911 Revolution, the Manchu dynasty was governed by provincial Viceroys. They were hated by the peasants. This picture shows some of the viceroys, ousted from their positions, being escorted onto a train by an armed guard.

the towns, for people had not yet learnt that China, weakened by years of corruption and mismanagement, could not be cured by a single act. Within months Sun had been ousted by Yuan Shih-k'ai. Yuan was quite incapable of dealing with the massive task of reconstruction, and he was followed by a succession of feeble "presidents". In the provinces, powerful landlords joined forces with army officers and made little Manchus of themselves. Private wars and banditry were the result, and the unlucky Chinese peasants found their position worse than ever, for they paid for every disaster.

Sun in Canton

Sun saw how far things had gone awry and again attempted to right China through revolution. With the help of the Russians he was able to gain control of Canton. He spent most of the rest of his life as head of the Canton government. He improved the city's amenities, gave legal equality to women and brought large areas of land into public ownership. Here he put into practice some of the reforms he had hoped to introduce into the whole of China. Sun died in 1925. His revolution had failed, but his hope and vision inspired the fighters who came after him.

▲ Yuan Shih-kai and Sun were the chief rivals for power within China from 1912–16. Yuan, a man with a flair for administration, was President of the new republic from 1912–16. He schemed to become Emperor, but was thwarted by a peasant rebellion led by Sun.

▲ Civil war continued after 1912 between forces led by Yuan Shih-kai and those led by the Nationalists, including Sun. In 1913 Yuan dismissed three Nationalist governors in the south. They, and other rulers, declared their independence, for they believed Yuan had betrayed the republic. Yuan's well-equipped army marched south and crushed this rebellion. Yuan then schemed to become emperor, but his plans came to nothing, for the Nationalist revolutionaries and Sun prevented him from establishing control.

▲ The first Chinese republic was proclaimed at Nanking. Sun is seen here at the announcement, in the middle of the first row (wearing a black coat).

▼ The Revolution finally erupted with great ferocity in 1911. An attack was made on Wuchang. Prisoners were rounded up for beheading and their bodies left to rot.

▲ Sun's mausoleum was built in Nanking after his death in 1925 and his body was finally laid to rest there in 1930. It is now a major centre for pilgrimage.

Mao Tse-tung and the new China

The maker of modern China

Dr. Sun's successor, Chiang Kai-shek, extended the Canton government's control over most of China. This government (the Kuomintang) built many new roads, repaired dams and bridges and introduced a modern banking system. However, it couldn't control the strong-arm landlords who had become dictators in the provinces. These landlords would imprison or kill peasants, they demanded huge taxes, sometimes 60 years in advance, and they conscripted peasants to fight in private wars.

Mao-Tse-tung, the son of peasants, was the maker of today's China. He believed that China would never recover until the peasants had been freed. Mao was born in 1893 in the village of Shaoshan. As a young man he divided his time between study and revolution. He was a founder of the Fourth Red Army, and devised its strategy. He became leader of the Chinese Communist Party during the Long March. At night, while the soldiers camped in caves or on snowy mountain slopes, Mao would retire to think and write. Here he created a new socialist philosophy based on the peasantry.

After the Second World War, civil war broke out again between Mao's forces and Chiang Kai-shek's army. Chiang's soldiers had been exhausted by the war with Japan, and inflation on a terrible scale had reduced wage-earners to destitution. In two years, prices doubled 67 times. The peasants flocked to Mao's standard, and soon even Chiang's soldiers were joining the communists. In 1949 Chiang fled to Formosa, and Mao declared the People's Republic of China.

The People's Republic

Mao set to work immediately rooting out the warlords, building schools, roads, irrigation schemes and industries. The land was given to the peasants, and many landlords fled. Others were imprisoned or executed. The retribution was severe, but it put China on its feet again.

Mao has remained leader of China since 1949, though there have been power struggles and attempts to oust him. Today he is old, and revered by the Chinese.

◀ Mao has always been a major military figure as well as a political one. The eventual success of the revolution was based on his mastery of fluid guerrilla tactics and his brilliantly imaginative strategy.

The route of the Long March

Occupied by Japan 1937

MANCHUKUO

KOREA

JAPAN

CHINA

KANSU

Yenan

Sian

SHENSI

SZECHWAN

R.Tatu

KWEICHOW

HUNAN

THE LONG MARCH 1934-35

KIANGSI

Occupied by Japan 1944

Scale 0 500 1000 km

▲ Mao served a long apprenticeship in the infant Chinese Communist Party of the 1920s where he developed his ideas of a peasant-based socialism. His early activities have since been depicted in portraits like these.

▼ In the 1946—9 civil war, the Kuomintang, despite their numerical superiority, were no match for the disciplined tactics of the P.L.A. Here a P.L.A. force is shown attacking Kuomintang troops in Chinchow.

▲ Chiang Kai-shek was leader of China during the Second World War. He was a very able politician, but was unable to rescue a corrupt regime from the control of foreigners.

► Statues of Mao in different attitudes are now commonplace in towns throughout China. But no roads or streets are named after him, on his orders.

The Cultural Revolution

The struggle for minds

The Great Proletarian Cultural Revolution erupted on the campus at Peking university in July 1966, and lasted until 1970. It was a huge struggle for minds which decided the course of China's development.

By 1965 China had come a long way since the Communist Party gained control of a demoralized, starving nation in 1949. Many people were beginning to forget the old hardship, to lose their revolutionary zeal, and writers sometimes included veiled criticism of the leadership in their plays and stories. Inside the Party itself there was a division. One group wanted to put the modernization of China first; their opponents called them "bourgeois materialists". Others, led by Mao, thought that the moral qualities of Spartan living combined with great dedication to the ideals of the revolution were the first priority. Their opponents called them "ultra-leftists".

The Red Guards

The Peking students rebelled against their teachers and the syllabus. Soon the revolt spread to the middle schools, and millions of students joined Red Guard brigades to attack "bourgeois materialism". Schools and universities were closed and Red Guards travelled all over the country attending mass meetings. They marched, singing, and addressed workers and peasants. Two years of confusion followed. There were some outbreaks of violence when groups of Red Guards with different views clashed with each other. Some dragged officials through the streets or kidnapped cabinet ministers. Wall-posters appeared in great profusion, giving contradictory advice. Foreign observers thought China was on the brink of civil war, but in fact the P.L.A. (the army) was always ready to step in to support Mao's group if things went awry. By 1968 the combat period was over. Schools and factories were re-opened, and the Communist Party Committee, purged of its "bourgeois materialists", decided to disband the Red Guards.

Many Red Guards were sent out to the underpopulated backlands of China to put their revolutionary theories into practice by working the land. School and university syllabuses became more political and foreign art and literature were suppressed. They were replaced by popular operas and ballets designed to entertain people and instruct them at the same time.

Inside the leadership, the Cultural Revolution left Mao firmly in command.

▼ During the Cultural Revolution, the Army supported the Maoists and helped Mao to emerge victorious. This picture was taken at a rally in Peking Workers' Stadium, 1967.

▲ Liu Shao-chi was one of the founders of the trade union movement in China and a veteran of the Chinese Communist Party. He was President of China from 1959–68. He was discredited by the Red Guards.

▲ The Army rallies in Shanghai, January 1967, in support of the Cultural Revolution. Shanghai was one of the main centres of the upheaval. Chiang Ching, Mao's wife, was the leader of the radicals in the city.

▼ *Dazibao*, big-character posters or wall newspapers, were used extensively by both sides during the Cultural Revolution. Leading personalities on both sides were denounced and both sides' policies were vigorously advocated. These posters criticised Liu Shao-chi and his "bourgeois materialism".

▲ Lin Piao was designated as Mao's successor as Party leader at the Ninth Party Congress in 1969. As Minister of Defence and commander-in-chief of the P.L.A., his future seemed assured. But, in 1971, he led an army-based coup against Mao. He was unsuccessful and died in an air crash while fleeing to Moscow. His clash with Mao has now been officially called a "two-line struggle"; its real nature is uncertain.

A genius for invention

▶ An early Chinese magnetic compass. It was invented by the Chinese and first used in the third century A.D. Before being used for marine navigation it was used by priests to calculate the correct position of buildings and tombs. The compass gave the Chinese a great advantage in trading.

▼ Paper and ink were invented by the Chinese at the end of the third century B.C. Paper was made from bamboo which was soaked and made into a pulp.

Inventions of ancient times

Chinese technology was advanced at the time Stonehenge was begun in Britain. The Chinese then used ploughs, studied astronomy, manufactured fine silk, and were skilled in the art of map-drawing.

Many things we now take for granted were first made and used in China: paper and printing, gunpowder, the breast-girth harness for horses, oars on boats and the stern-post rudder. The Chinese first thought of water-wheels for grinding corn, the double-acting piston bellows, and some interesting aeronautic devices, like the kite.

Writing and printing

Writing, paper and printing are very important developments in any civilization. Chinese script is possibly the world's oldest and has changed so little that scholars can read manuscripts more than a thousand years old without difficulty.

The first writing was cut into slips of bamboo until ink and paper were invented in the third century B.C. Printing, the next big advance, came in the eighth century A.D. As cheaper printed books became available, more people learned to read and write, and the study of philosophy, history and literature developed.

3   *2*   *1*

▲ The use of rudders attached to the stern of ships was a Chinese invention of the eighth century A.D. This simple device replaced the steering oar which was heavier and difficult to manoeuvre. All ships today have such rudders.

► Silk-making was invented, according to legend, by the Empress Si-Liz about 2640 B.C. Its popularity made it a major item of trade with the West for many centuries. Chinese silks are still made for export.

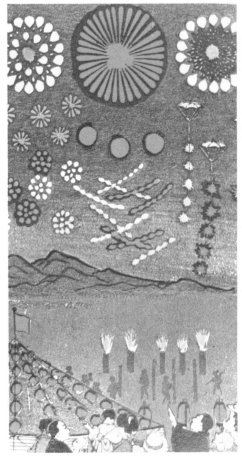

▲ A Chinese scroll, called the Diamond Sutra, is one of the earliest examples of printing (A.D. 868). It was printed by carving Chinese characters out of pieces of wood. Ink was spread on the wood blocks and then pressed onto the paper. The blocks could be used again whenever the same character was needed. The illustration was carved especially for the scroll.

► Simple fireworks were described in Chinese literature as early as 600 A.D. Gunpowder (sulphur, charcoal and salt-petre) was known to the Chinese by about A.D. 1000. It was used to propel rockets by 1100, and fireworks have remained a part of the Chinese tradition. In addition gunpowder was used in warfare for cannons. The first bronze cannon was cast in 1332.

Custom and superstition

The Spring Festival

Many ancient and fascinating customs survive in China. One is the tradition of naming years after twelve animals. These animals range from mythological beasts like the dragon and strange creatures like the serpent, to farmyard and domestic animals: the horse, sheep, chicken and dog. So 1974 became tiger year; 1975 the year of the horse, and in 1976 the dragon presides.

The years and the seasons are a vivid presence in a peasant society, and the Chinese calendars reflect this. The peasants still use an ancient calendar with 24 months named after the weather and the needs of farming. Newspapers always give the date on this ancient "Hsai calendar". In the towns, a twelve-month calendar is followed. On both calendars the year begins dramatically with new year celebrations, the Spring Festival. This falls in late January or early February. Most people have three days' holiday to welcome the new year, and every nationality celebrates it in traditional style, with colourful costume, dancing and singing. Meetings are held in the open air, and political leaders exhort the people to make good use of the new-born year just given to them.

Dragons and vampires

Folk tales of monsters—some good, some evil—abound in China. Chinese vampires, for instance, have glaring eyes, long sharp claws and bodies covered in greenish-white hair. They do nobody any good, but dragons are kindly monsters, unless provoked. Trees occupy an important place in mythology, for people believed they had souls and once worshipped them. Trees in traditional painting are represented with especial delicacy, for they rose out of the earth towards heaven, and are beautiful in the costume of every season.

The communist government has been quite practical about ancient customs and superstitions. Folklore is part of the national culture so, unless beliefs are positively harmful, the government does not interfere with them.

▲ In Christian art, the dragon is a symbol of sin and paganism, but in China the dragon has a quite a different symbolic meaning. The dragon, unicorn, phoenix and turtle are the four benevolent spiritual animals and the dragon is the most important. Later the dragon became the emperor's special symbol. The dragon symbolizes energy, law, masculinity, good magic and the teaching of the art of painting.

▲ May Day is an important national holiday, and is celebrated with parades and festivities. People wear gay clothes, and dance in colourful formations.

▲ At the height of the Cultural Revolution, in 1967, Mao took a nine-mile swim in the river Yangtse. This was widely publicized to encourage people to keep fit.

◄ People of all ages get up early in the morning to do calisthenic exercises. The sidewalks are filled with people busy at the task of keeping fit.

▼ Tea is the Chinese national drink, and the taking of tea on formal occasions is accompanied by ceremony. This picture shows a foreign visitor invited to tea by a group of Chinese leaders. As the guest enters, the hosts stand up and clap to welcome him.

Looking into the future

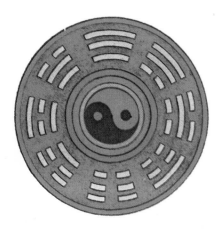

The Chinese have had a long tradition for attempting to foretell the future. The most famous method was set down in a book named the *I Ching* or *Book of Changes*. The circular diagram above is part of it. The inner design is an ancient symbol of the harmony of opposites and is widely used as a good luck charm over doorways and on jewellery. Each of the groups of lines on the outside have names and a significance. Using a complex ritual involving their arrangement, future trends are said to be foretold.

The Chinese character

Some Chinese characteristics

▲ In China, comradeship and friendship are valued. People are expected to be thoughtful and affectionate, and they usually are.

▲ The Chinese work extremely hard. The hours are long, the holidays few. A sense of community spirit carries them through.

▼ What do the Chinese people think of themselves? Generally, they think the Chinese are a positive, warm, proud, loyal people and rather like being Chinese.

▲ The old are honoured in Chinese culture and their views are listened to with respect. They usually live with their children and grandchildren.

▲ Ideology influences every aspect of Chinese life. There are pictures of Mao in many homes, and people study his writings.

The paradoxical Chinese

The Chinese are paradoxical. They are very conservative in many of their habits and outlook. Yet they are willing participants in the most far-reaching socialist experiment that has ever taken place.

They are extremely proud of what they have managed to achieve since 1949. But this pride has its negative aspects. Many Chinese think of themselves as a superior race, particularly in relation to other Asian people.

This pride also leads them into insularity. The Chinese speak in favour of international co-operation. But few of them seem interested in anything that happens outside of China, unless it affects them directly. This of course is partly the fault of other nations, which have been very hostile to China. Things are now slowly beginning to change.

The community spirit

The Chinese think of themselves as diligent, hard-working and disciplined. They do have these qualities, but not quite as much of them as they think and Westerners accept.

◄ These two friends pose proudly while the photographer snaps them. The simple pleasures of a day out in the open are much appreciated by the Chinese.

On the whole, they work efficiently rather than hard.

Chinese people are friendly and care for their fellows, creating a community spirit that is hardly known in the West. They are also welcoming and extremely polite to foreigners. But the very elaborate courtesy they display may mean they don't quite trust foreigners.

On the surface they are placid and easy-going. But underneath they tend to bottle up their anger and frustrations and let them out in one big orgy of destruction. This sometimes happened during the Cultural Revolution.

They have a quiet, sly sense of humour and will gently poke fun at absurd behaviour or excess. Linked with this is a strong sense of propriety. The Chinese follow a strict code of sexual morality. They disapprove of sex before marriage, and consider prostitution to be utterly degrading.

Overall they are very self-confident, secure in their belief that their country occupies an important place among nations, and that China has much to offer other countries.

▲ These people, on a commune near Tsingtao in Shantung province, are making nets for the next fishing season. All productive work is regarded as honourable under the socialist creed of China, and these fisherfolk take pride in their skill.

◄ The Chinese think that people should be sufficiently sure of themselves to be able to relax anywhere. This man is taking things easy during a break from work, relaxing with tea and a Chinese cigarette.

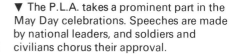

▼ The P.L.A. takes a prominent part in the May Day celebrations. Speeches are made by national leaders, and soldiers and civilians chorus their approval.

▲ Children in procession before giving a display of singing and dancing at a children's cultural palace. They hope to attract people to come back to watch.

How China is changing

The rebirth of China

The twentieth century has changed the face of the world. Among all this upheaval and new birth, China stands out as the country which has the widest transformation. A corrupt and hopelessly inefficient imperial despotism was followed by a republic which degenerated into near-chaos, itself followed by a failed attempt at Western style administration. Then came the communist revolution. Since then Chinese society has been completely remade, and China has followed a different course from any other nation. The changes have affected not only the face, but the very soul of China. A stroll through a street in any town will give indications: everybody has enough to eat, but nobody has luxuries; everybody wears a worker's uniform; ordinary people revere their political leaders in an astonishingly

◄ China surprised the world by launching its first low grade nuclear bomb in 1964. Ten further atomic tests followed.

► As part of a drive to make Chinese people aware of their international responsibilities thousands of posters like these are on billboards everywhere.

▼ The friendship between China and the U.S.S.R. ended in 1960, when Khrushchev, the Soviet leader, withdrew all Russian advisers. There have since been several border incidents. Chinese and Soviet troops are seen here arguing in China's Chenpao Island area.

innocent way; theft is almost unheard of; tiny neat flats replace hideous slums.

China and the World

China's foreign policy has changed equally dramatically. In the first years after the revolution, Russia assisted the Chinese, but lately relations between China and the Soviet Union have deteriorated. In the north, China shares a border with the far eastern soviets, and trouble is frequent.

The Chinese have recently extended a friendly hand to the United States and Europe. The visits of Western politicians have been accompanied by an increase in trade. China now has a seat in the United Nations, and takes part in international sporting activities.

China is also making a contribution towards assisting poorer countries. China's

homespun expertise is especially useful.

Behind the scenes more changes are on the way. The huge burst of effort to remake China has come from its leaders, and within the leadership political struggles are as common as in any country. The Cultural Revolution was one leadership struggle which broke out into the streets, and it showed that the stability of China is precarious. Mao's amazing visionary leadership must end soon, for Mao is a very old man. Middle-aged people, who have seen enough of the bad old days are grateful for the changes, but the new generation expect more. China needs bigger industries. These industries are generators of wealth and power. They may well weaken agriculture and the strength of the peasantry. Yet the peasantry are the heart of China's communism, and their future is China's future.

New directions for the Chinese

▲ As a means of cutting down China's birthrate, late marriage (28 for men, 26 for women) is now officially encouraged. The law permits earlier marriage.

▲ China is slowly emerging into the international sports arena. Her national games are table tennis, basketball, volleyball and now also football.

▶ The Chinese standard of living has greatly improved since 1949. Medicine, education and housing are areas where people have particularly benefited.

▲ President Nixon and Henry Kissinger visited China in 1972, for discussions with Chinese leaders. This was the first official contact between China and the U.S.A. since the revolution. Since then, relations have become quite cordial.

Reference
Physical and Human Geography

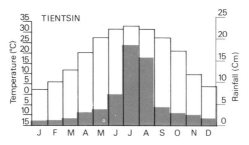

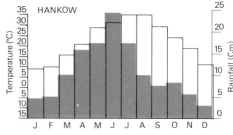

China experiences almost every type of climate from the high cold mountain areas of Tibet to the hot deserts of Sinkiang, to the temperate and sub-tropical monsoons of China proper. The North is liable to severe drought while the South-east coasts can receive rainfall in excess of 2,000 mm per year. Coastal regions from Shanghai to Hainan are prone to typhoons.

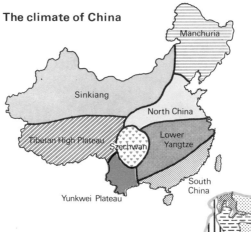

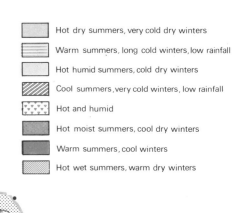

The climate of China

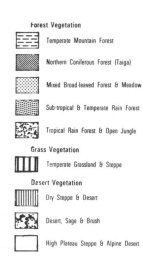

Hot dry summers, very cold dry winters

Warm summers, long cold winters, low rainfall

Hot humid summers, cold dry winters

Cool summers, very cold winters, low rainfall

Hot and humid

Hot moist summers, cool dry winters

Warm summers, cool winters

Hot wet summers, warm dry winters

The natural vegetation of China

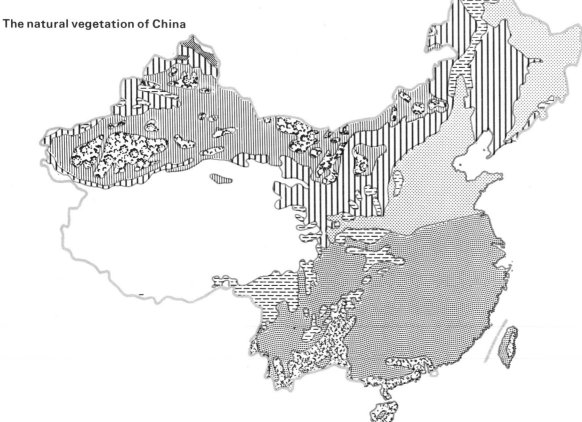

Forest Vegetation

Temperate Mountain Forest

Northern Coniferous Forest (Taiga)

Mixed Broad-leaved Forest & Meadow

Sub-tropical & Temperate Rain Forest

Tropical Rain Forest & Open Jungle

Grass Vegetation

Temperate Grassland & Steppe

Desert Vegetation

Dry Steppe & Desert

Desert, Sage & Brush

High Plateau Steppe & Alpine Desert

Populations of principal cities

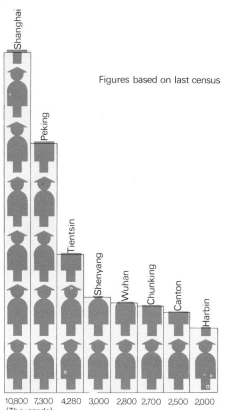

Figures based on last census

Shanghai	Peking	Tientsin	Shenyang	Wuhan	Chunking	Canton	Harbin
10,800 (Thousands)	7,300	4,280	3,000	2,800	2,700	2,500	2,000

The population density

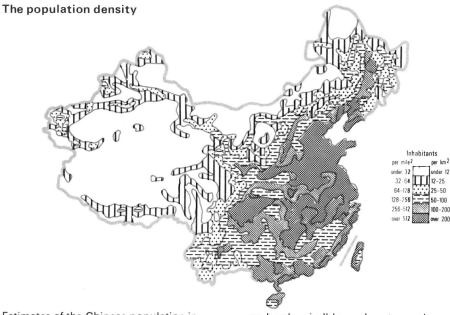

Inhabitants

per mile²	per km²
under 32	under 12
32–64	12–25
64–128	25–50
128–256	50–100
256–512	100–200
over 512	over 200

Estimates of the Chinese population in 1974/5 vary from 750 to 850 million. There are probably about 800 million people living in China today, which makes China the most populous nation on earth.

The latest reliable census was carried out in 1953. It revealed that of the 582,603,417 people in China at that time, only 22,466,101 lived in the huge territories in the north, west and centre of China. Many of these territories are harsh, windblown desert or rocky mountains.

In 1953, nearly 87 per cent of the population lived in rural areas. Men outnumbered women by 107 to 100.

Today the government is making efforts to encourage people to limit their families. There are birth control clinics in every town, and late marriage is encouraged. So far these campaigns have had little success.

China is a communist state, but the party has no actual position in the constitution. Its complete dominance over government is possible by ensuring that all positions in government from local to national levels are filled by party members. In 1965 it was estimated that only 18 million were members of the party.

In the constitution the highest organ of authority is the National People's Congress (N.P.C.). It is composed of deputies elected by the provinces, the autonomous regions, municipalities and the People's Liberation Army. It decides the national economic plan, enacts laws, appoints officials, etc. The executive and administrative functions of government are carried out by the State Council which is headed by the Premier and his ministers. Below the State Council are Provincial Revolutionary Committees (composed of representatives from the cadres, the masses and the P.L.A.). Below the Provincial Committees are similarly composed Revolutionary Committees to be found at all levels of local government.

The Communist party has a similar structure to the N.P.C. and, as all officials are members of the Communist party, the decisions made at party congresses dictate the decisions to be made by the N.P.C. A central committee is elected by the congress for five years.

The government of China depends largely on the leadership of the chairman of the Communist party, Mao Tse-tung.

The Chinese system of government

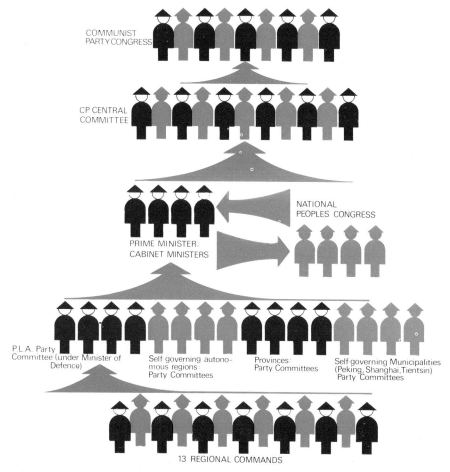

COMMUNIST PARTY CONGRESS

CP CENTRAL COMMITTEE

NATIONAL PEOPLES CONGRESS

PRIME MINISTER: CABINET MINISTERS

P.L.A. Party Committee (under Minister of Defence)

Self-governing autonomous regions: Party Committees

Provinces: Party Committees

Self-governing Municipalities (Peking, Shanghai, Tientsin) Party Committees

13 REGIONAL COMMANDS

Reference
History

MAIN EVENTS IN CHINESE HISTORY

B.C.

c.2200	Supposed founding of Hsai dynasty.
c.1700	Probable beginning of Shang dynasty.
1054	Wu Wang and army officers topple Shang dynasty and execute last Shang king. Chou dynasty begins.
c.1000	Silk weaving, ploughing, astronomy and map drawing begin.
c.770	China becomes known as "Chung Kuo", meaning "Middle Kingdom" or "Centre Country".
551-479	Life of Confucius.
278	Soldiers of Ch'in seize the Chou capital.
255	Ch'in soldiers gain control of China.
221	Shih Huang Ti ("First Emperor") completes the Ch'in conquest of China.
c.200	Great Wall of China replaces ancient walls.
206	First Peasant Rising led by Lui Pang (minor official of peasant stock) overthrows Ch'in organization. Lui Pang becomes first Han emperor.
206-195	Kao Tsu centralizes government under a class of mandarins, or provincial governors.
c.200	Paper and ink invented.
141	Programme of canal-building begins.
124	Imperial University founded for the study of Confucian classics.
111	Vietnam conquered by China.

A.D.

75-100	Buddhism spreads in north China.
220-581	Period of many civil wars and national disunity.
641	A Chinese princess introduces Buddhism to Tibet.
c.700	Printing invented.
8-900	Newspapers produced, printed books appeared, the first encyclopaedia.
1215	Capture of Peking by Genghis Khan.
1271	Marco Polo's first visit to China.
1279-1368	Mongol or Ch'ing dynasty. Expeditions sent to discover the source of Yellow River. Observatory founded. New calendar based on 365-day year introduced.
1368	Chu-Yuan chang, a former Buddhist novice of peasant origins organizes a rebellion against the Mongols and expels them.
1405	Cheng Ho's first naval expedition to Malaya, India and Africa.
1644	Manchus conquer Peking and establish the Ch'ing or Manchu dynasty.
1683	Manchus conquer Taiwan.
1670-1750	Manchus conquer Turkestan and Tibet.
1839	British traders ignore Manchu regulations; China declares war, the Opium War.
1842-3	Treaty of Nanking ends Opium War. Britain gains Hong Kong and access to Chinese ports.
1850	Taiping rebellion breaks out — a religious, communist type revolution of peasants and intellectuals against the Manchus.
1853	Taipings capture Nanking.
1856	"Arrow War", the second war with Western trading countries, breaks out.
1857	British and French troops occupy Canton.
1858	China defeated. Treaties with Britain, France, Russia and the U.S.A. allow them special trade privileges.
1860	Manchus withdraw these privileges; British and French occupy Peking.
1862	Prince Kuang attempts to reform the weakened and demoralized Manchus: he is ousted by his aunt, the Empress Dowager Tz'u Hsi.
1864	Taipings defeated in Nanking and the rebellion ends.
1870	Massacre of foreigners in Tientsin.
1871	Russian troops invade Sinkiang.
1884	War with France. French take Annam.
1887	Portugal takes Amoy.
1892	Sun Yat-sen founds the China Resurrection Society.
1894	War with Japan.
1895	China crushingly defeated by Japan. Japanese take Taiwan, Liaotung and gain concessions in China.
1896	Foreigners build railways in China, introduce their own gunboats and police.
1897	Dairen occupied by Russians.
1898	Boxers ("Society of Righteous and Harmonious Fists") became skilled in ancient arts of self-defence, and march under the slogan "Overthrow the Ch'ing and expel the barbarians".
1899	Boxer rebellion spreads rapidly.
1900	Boxers beseige eleven foreign legations in Peking. China forced to pay £265m. compensation.
1905	Sun Yat-sen organises the anti-Manchu movement from Japan.
1911	Revolution breaks out in Wuhan. Manchu dynasty overthrown.
1911	Sun Yat-sen declares the Chinese republic. The Manchus flee.
1913	Yuan Shih-k'ai becomes president.
1915	Japan presents "Twenty One Demands" to China.
1916	Yuan dies. Provincial governors declare their independence. Period of disunity and warlordism begins.
1919	Violent outbreaks against Japanese power in China. First general strike.
1920	Strike of Manchurian railway workers. Ch'en Tu-hsiu (the "Father of Chinese Communism") founds the Chinese Socialist Youth League.
1921	Chinese Communist Party founded.
1923	Russians aid Koumintang.
1925	Sun Yat-sen dies of cancer.
1926	Peasant communism spreads. Chiang Kai-shek and his Kuomintang government quarrel with the communists.
1927	Chiang massacres communists in Shanghai, then sends soldiers against communists in the country. Mao Tse-tung leads a peasant uprising in Hunan. Creation of Fourth Red Army.
1928	Mao Tse-tung and Chu Teh gain control of Kiangsi. They reform farming and educate the peasants.
1930	Chiang Kai-shek launches his first "bandit extermination" campaign against the communist groups.
1931	Manchuria occupied by Japan.
1933	Fifth "bandit extermination" campaign. 60,000 Red Army soldiers and about one million peasants die.
1934	Chiang completes all-out attack on the Red Army. Communists retreat. Long March begins.
1935	Mao gains control of the Communist Party. Red Army reaches northern Shensi with 20,000 survivors.
1937	Chiang and communists agree to work together against Japanese invaders.
1938	Japanese occupy large areas of China.
1939	Second World War breaks out. Japanese circulate worthless paper money, starting a spiral of inflation.
1943	Early "communes" formed in communist-controlled areas of China.
1945	Civil war between communists and Chiang's Kuomintang government breaks out again. Russia occupies Manchuria.
1946	Full scale civil war. Terrible inflation; millions become destitute and die of starvation.
1947	Kuomintang gains Yenan; communists increase control.
1948	U.S.A. backs Kuomintang. Chiang's capital, Nanking, falls to the communists.
1949	Many Kuomintang soldiers go over to the communists. Communists take Peking and most of mainland China. Chiang Kai-shek and the last of his army are ferried to the island of Formosa. Mao Tse-tung declares the People's Republic of China.
1950	Chinese "volunteers" fight U.N. troops in Korean war.

1956 "Hundred flowers" campaign.
-7 Criticism of régime encouraged and then repressed.
1958 "Great Leap Forward". Great efforts to increase industrial production. Communes formed.
1962 Border skirmished with India.
1963 Split with Russia becomes open opposition.
1966 Cultural Revolution begins. Struggle for leadership of China. Liu Shao-chi discredited by Red Guards.
1967 First atomic bomb exploded.
1971 Lin Pao killed in air crash after alleged coup against Mao.
1972 President Nixon visits China.

THE MAJOR DYNASTIES OF CHINESE RULERS
Shang (c. 1700-1054 B.C.)
An agricultural society headed by a king and court. Had silk, a highly developed script of 2,500 characters, bronze vessels, jade carvings; used wheeled chariots for war; had elaborate town-planning.
Chou (1054-256 B.C.)
Created the feudal system. Agriculture, schools and literature flourished. Confucius and other sages lived in this period. Taoism began.
Ch'in (255-206 B.C.)
Replaced feudalism by military government. Excellent horsemen. Extended the Great Wall. Standardized the Chinese script. reorganized the system of weights and measures. Created a scholar gentry.
Han (206 B.C.—220 A.D.)
Developed an efficient civil service. Introduced examinations. Buddhism came to China from Central Asia. Musical notation developed. Trade, art and literature flourished.
(300 years of disunity and civil war followed)
Sui (581-618 A.D.)
Reunited China. Built a great network of roads.
T'ang (618-906 A.D.)
Government became efficient and China became politically powerful. Literature, painting and music flourished. Printing techniques developed. China was the most advanced country in the world by 900 A.D.
Sung (960-1279 A.D.)
Fine porcelain and landscape paintings.
Mongol (or Yuan) (1279-1368 A.D.)
Destroyed much of the art and scholarship of the past. Genghis Khan conquered the north, and Kublai Khan created a vast empire stretching across Asia. Trade flourished. The Chinese hated the Mongols as foreign oppressors.
Ming (1368-1644 A.D.)
Begun by a former Buddhist novice. Chinese culture recovered. Great novels and poetry. Ming ceramics became world-famous.
Manchu (Ch'ing) (1694-1911)
The Manchus invaded from the north. Adopted Chinese culture. Their later years were bedevilled by pressure from foreign powers.

The Arts

The great periods of Chinese art
Han dynasty (206 B.C.-220 A.D.): bronze mirrors, weapons, chariot fittings and vessels. Jades. Lead glazed pottery. Pottery tomb figures. Lacquer cups and boxes. Tomb wall paintings.
T'ang dynasty (618-906 A.D.): Pottery tomb figures. Wall and scroll paintings of figures, court scenes, horses and Buddhist subjects. White and green glazed porcelain. Silverware and gold ornaments. Noted painters include: Han Kan (c.750), famed for his horses; Wu Tao-tzu (700-760) who painted demons, dragons and saints on temple walls; and Yen Li-pen (640-680), a portrait painter of scholars and famous men, *Thirteen emperors*.
Sung dynasty (960-1279 A.D.): scroll, screen, album and fan paintings of landscapes, figures, flowers and birds. First ink landscape painting. Porcelain with celadon and other monochrome glazes. Silver, lacquer and jade. Painters include Li Ch'eng (940-990), greatest of Chinese landscape painters; Ma Yuan (1150-1230), *Walking on a Mountain in Spring, A Scholar and His Servant on a Terrace*.
Mongol dynasty (1279-1367): figure and horse paintings at the Mongol court. Ink landscape paintings by scholarly recluses. The first blue-and-white and copper-red underglaze porcelain. Lacquer and silver. Painters include Ni Tsan (1301-1374), landscapist known for his simple style, *Trees in a River at Yu-shan*; Sheng Mou (1310-1361) noted for landscapes with delicate lines and touches of colour.
Ming dynasty (1368-1644): Blue-and-white porcelain. Porcelain enamelled in many colours. Lacquer and silver. Scroll, album and fan paintings of landscapes and figures. Painters include: Wen Cheng-ming (1470-1559), landscapes of austere and sombre qualities, *Old Trees by a Cold Waterfall*; Lu Chi, most famous bird and flower painter at Ming Court, *Geese by a Snowy Bank*.
Ch'ing dynasty (1644-1911): Multi-coloured porcelain. Scroll, album and fan paintings of landscapes and figures. Painters include: Chu Ta (1625-1705) painter of powerful landscapes and glowering birds and fish.

LITERATURE
Confucian Classics (c.500-202 B.C.): Writings of Confucius and followers, *Book of Documents, Book of Changes, Book of Poetry, Book of Rites, Spring and Autumn Analects*. Vast influence on all later Chinese writing and thought.
Ssu-ma Ch'ien (179-117 B.C.): wrote first official history of China, *Historical Records*.
Lu Chi (261-303 A.D.): wrote first analysis of the art of writing, *Essay on Literature*.

T'ao Ch'ien (365-427 A.D.): one of China's greatest poets. A recluse who lived most of his life on a small farm.
Li Po (701-762): Great poet of T'ang dynasty, *Night Thoughts, The Song of Wine*.
Tu Fu (712-770): Poet and founder of realistic school of poetry.
Po Chu-i (772-846): Governor of Honan province and writer of famous ballads and lyrics, *The Everlasting Sorrow*.
Ssu-ma Kung (1019-1086): author of *Comprehensive Mirror for Aid in Governing*, a history of China from the 5th century A.D. to 959 A.D.
Kao Ch'i (1336-1374): great Ming poet, The *Earthen Pot Resounds*.
Wu Ch'eng-en (c.1500-1580): novelist, *Record of Journey to the West* (translated in English as *Monkey*).
P'u Sung-ling (1640-1715): author of collection of tales, *Strange Stories*, on supernatural themes.
Ts'ao Chan and **Kao E** (18th century): authors of *Dream of the Red Chamber*, novel about a great family and a protest against convention.
Liu E (1857-1909): *The Travels of Lao-ts'an*, a novel which looked at the uncertain future of China.
Lu Hsun (1881-1936): wrote classic of modern Chinese fiction, *The Story of Ah Q*.
Mao Tun (1896-): Novelist much influenced by the West, *The Eclipse, Rainbow, The Twilight*.
Ts'ao Yu (1910-): playwright, *The Thunderstorm, Sunrise*.

PHILOSPHERS AND THINKERS
Lao Tzu (6th century B.C.): traditional founder of philosophy of Taoism and alleged author of *Tao Te ching* (Scripture of the way and the Power) which is source book of Taoism.
Confucius (551-479 B.C.): Founder of major philosophy which puts forward the necessity for morality, duty, manners and rituals. Wrote *the Analects*. Had huge influence on later China and his ideas are still under discussion today.
Menicus (c.372-289 B.C.): Follower of Confucius who believed that goodness of man is the source of good government.
Hsun Tzu (300-327 B.C.): Disciple of Confucius who thought that man is naturally evil and liable to change.
Han Fei T'zu (died 233 B.C.): Favoured ruthless totalitarian rule as a means to government.
Wang Yang-ming (1472-1529): Confucianist who thought man's mind is the centre of the universe.
K'ang Yu-wei (1858-1927): Political reformer who used Confucianism as a reason for political change.
Sun Yat-sen (1866-1925): Father of the Chinese revolution. Thought in his book, *Three Principles of the People*.

Mao Tse-tung (1893-): chief architect of modern China. His *Thoughts* have become the guiding light for today's China.

Reference
The Economy

Some Chinese exports

Food products

Silk wool cotton

Pottery and porcelain

Industrial materials

Main sources of income:
Agriculture: wheat, barley, maize, millet, soya beans, rice, tea, cotton, hemp, jute, flax, tobacco, pigs, silk, timber.
Industry: textiles, steel, chemicals, cement, agricultural equipment, plastics, lorries.
Mining: China has vast mineral resources. Coal, iron, oil, tin, tungsten, manganese, antimony, molybdenum.

Main trading partners: Japan, Hong Kong, West Germany, U.S.S.R., Britain, Cuba.

Currency: Unit of currency is the Yuan (or PBY), which is divided into 10 chiao; the chiao divided into 10 fen. Official rate of exchange is £1 = PBY 5.9 or U.S. $1.00 = PBY 2.46.

Chinese imports and exports

China's trading activities have increased considerably since the Chinse ended their policy of isolation, around 1972.
Principal exports are animals and food products, seed oils, textiles, ores, metals and tea.
Imports include raw cotton, motor vehicles, machinery, chemical fertilizers, wheat, aircraft, paper, dyes and chemicals.

Standards of living

Standards of living in China have improved dramatically since 1949. Famine has been banished, inflation does not exist in China, and there is full employment. This is a real achievement when today's China is compared with other Asian countries, like India, and with the condition of China before the revolution.

However, the size of the population and its rate of increase, are likely to threaten future plans for improvement. By 1978, the population is likely to reach 1,000 million. At present 90 per cent of the population is concentrated into 15 per cent of the land. For the same land to feed a much greater population, vastly improved methods of agriculture will be needed. Better irrigation and more use of fertilizers will help towards a solution, but only in the short term.

Prospects for the future

More people will move to the cities as industrialization progresses. This may bring many of the problems which other industrialized nations know so well: inadequate housing, unemployment, rising food prices. China is, however, able to direct workers to places where labour is needed. The Chinese are aware of the need to conserve resources, both natural and human.

The Chinese decision to base national development on agriculture is a bold experiment which has been remarkably successful so far.

Agriculture in China

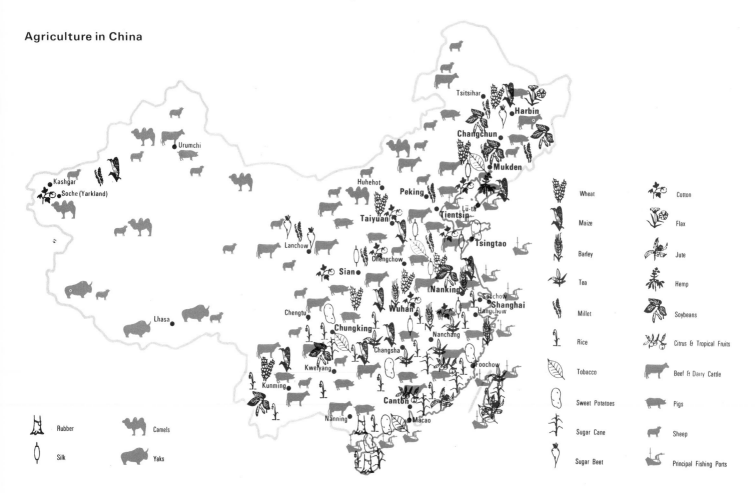

Industry in China

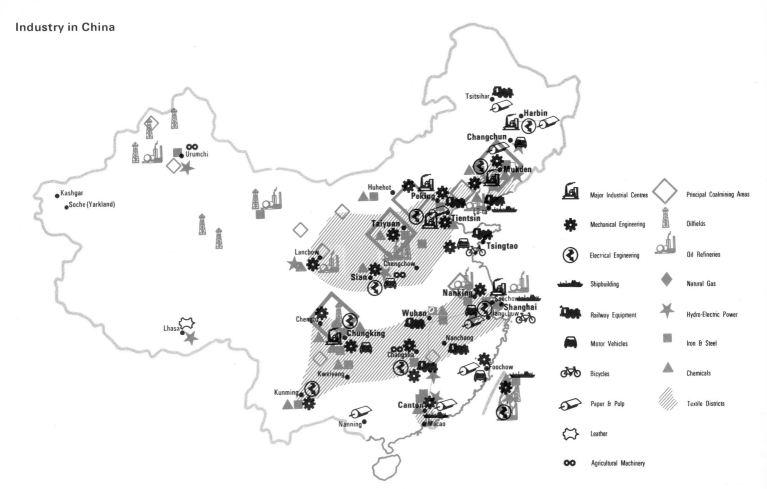

Legend:
- Major Industrial Centres
- Mechanical Engineering
- Electrical Engineering
- Shipbuilding
- Railway Equipment
- Motor Vehicles
- Bicycles
- Paper & Pulp
- Leather
- Agricultural Machinery
- Principal Coalmining Areas
- Oilfields
- Oil Refineries
- Natural Gas
- Hydro-Electric Power
- Iron & Steel
- Chemicals
- Textile Districts

Employment and productivity in China

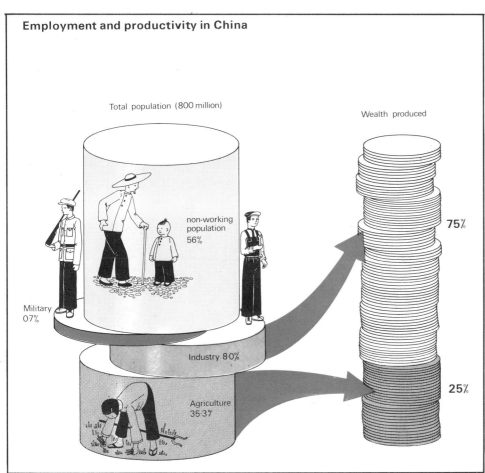

Total population (800 million)

Wealth produced

non-working population 56%

Military 07%

Industry 80%

Agriculture 353%

75%

25%

When the Communists took control in 1949, China lay shattered by war. A period of intense development took place. The first Five-Year Plan 1953–7 showed considerable gains in industry but agriculture was badly neglected.

During the second Five-Year Plan begun in 1958, both industrial and agricultural growth declined. Disasterous harvests in 1960–1, though partly due to bad weather, led to the import of wheat from Canada and Australia. Industrial planning during the Great Leap Forward (1958–61) was found to be misguided. Thousands of backyard iron-smelting furnaces and other tiny factories were set up to increase production. However the steel produced proved to be virtually useless. In addition, the withdrawal of Russian technical help in 1960 stopped production in many key industrial plants.

To recover her former rapid growth, plans were completely reversed. Agriculture was now seen as the key to development. The formation of communes in 1958 had given a sound basis for agriculture and by 1966 the communes had begun to work well. Heavy industrial production was diverted into manufacturing agricultural equipment. Today both agricultural and industrial growth is increasing though *per capita* output remains low and total production does not meet national requirements. China today is determined to be self-sufficient and is surprising the world by the speed with which she is developing advanced technology.

Gazetteer

Canton. 23 15N 113 30E. Now called Kwangchow by the Chinese. Situated on the Pearl or Canton River. Chief seaport, industrial and commercial centre of S. China with considerable river trade. As a result of the First Opium War (1839-42), it became one of the first treaty ports. Population: c. 2.5 million.

Changchun. 43 20N 126 30E. Railway junction on S. Manchurian Railway and capital of Kirin Province, N.E. China. Industrial centre (railway engineering, saw milling, food processing). Seat of the People's University of N.E. China (founded 1958).

Chengtu. 30 50N 104 5E. Capital of Szechwan Province, on the fertile Chengtu plain N.W. of Chungking. Commercial centre for trade between the mountainous region of N.W. Szechwan and the Red Basin, in an area irrigated by a system created in the 3rd century BC.

Chungking. 29 32N 106 45E. Important river port in Szechwan Province on the Yangtse River. Major iron and steel and manufacturing centre. Its history dates back to the Hsia dynasty, in the 3rd millenium BC. Wartime capital of China, 1937-46.

Foochow. 26 10N 119 20E. One of the original treaty ports after the Opium War in 1842. Situated in Fulkien Province in the S.E., it exports timber, bamboo shoots and sugar cane. Manufactures machinery, chemicals, textiles and paper.

Hangchow. 29 55N 120 15E. Situated in the maritime province of Chekiang. A commercial centre which trades in silk, tea and rice. Has two universities, founded in 1927 and 1959. Capital of S. China during the Sung Dynasty (12th century).

Harbin. 45 40N 126 40E. Capital of Heilungkiang Province in the N.E. Important industrial, commercial and route centre, founded by the Russians in 1897. Flour milling, soyabean processing, sugar-refining, railway engineering.

Hofei. 31 50N 117 0E. Capital of Anhwei Province in the East. Commercial centre in an agricultural region producing rice, tobacco and beans.

Hong Kong. 22 20N 114 10E. British colony on the coast of Kwangtung Province, S. China, consisting of Hong Kong Island, Stonecutters' Island, the ceded territory of Kowloon and the New Territory. Population 4 million (98 per cent Chinese). Entrepot port. Manufactures cotton goods, rubber footwear, ropes, cement and paint. British lease expires in 1997, when Hong Kong should revert to China.

Huhehot. 40 50N 111 20E. Capital of Inner Mongolia Autonomous Region. Population. c. 200,000. Industrial and commercial centre, manufacturing textiles, rugs, bricks and tiles. A Mongolian religious centre and seat of the Grand Lama until the 17th century.

Hwang Ho River. 39 0N 107E. Second longest river in China (2,900 miles long).

Nicknamed "China's Sorrow", because of the number of times it has changed course in the last 4,000 years. On the credit side, the silt it carries down has extended the delta and provided additional land for crops.

Inner Mongolia. 42 0N 111 0E. N.E. Autonomous Region. Area: 455,000 square miles. Population c. 11.5 million. Lies mainly in the Mongolian Plateau but rises in the E. to the Great Khingan Mountains and in the S. to the Ala Shan. Nomadic stock rearing, chiefly of sheep, goats, horses and camels, is the traditional occupation of the Mongolian people.

Kunming. 25 3N 102 40E. Commercial, cultural and route centre in Yunnan Province. The terminus of the Burma Road, with a population of c. 1.2 million.

Kwangsi-Chuang. 24 0N 107 30E. Autonomous Region. Situated in S. China, bordering on N. Vietnam. Its population of c. 22 million inhabits 85,000 square miles. It is generally hilly and occupies the basin of the upper Si-kiang River.

Kweiyuang. 26 50N 106 55E. Capital of Kweichow Province, a manufacturing centre and an important road junction. Manufactures iron and steel, textiles and chemicals.

Lanchow. 36 0N 109 0E. An important route, commercial and cultural centre in Kansu Province. The famous Silk Road to Sinkiang starts here, which is the centre of caravan trade with Tibet, India and the U.S.S.R.

Lhasa. 29 42N 91 10E. Capital of Tibet. Population 75,000. The chief centre of Lamaism and Tibet's main commercial centre. Trades in grain, wool, furs and tea. Dominated by the great Potala, formerly the official residence of the Dalai Lama. The Jokang Temple is in the centre of the city, an important point for Buddhist pilgrimage.

Macao. 22 15N 113 35E. Portuguese overseas province in S.E. China since 1557. Consists of the town of Macao and the small islands of Taipa and Coloane. Has a considerable transit trade with China and exports salted and fresh fish.

Nanchang. 28 22N 115 49E. Capital of Kwangsi Province, occupied by the Japanese in 1939-45 War. Commercial and industrial centre, trading in tea, rice, cotton, hemp and tobacco.

Nanking. 32 5N 118 55E. Capital of Kiangsu Province on the River Yangtse. A river port and industrial centre. Founded in 1368 on the site of an ancient city, it was made 'southern capital' by the first Ming emperor but was deserted for Peking in 1421. The Nationalist Government's capital from 1928-49. Notable for Sun Yat-sen's mausoleum and for the 2-decker road and rail bridge, completed in 1968.

Nanning. 22 50N 107 8E. Capital of Kwangsi-Chuang A.R. River port (on Siang River) trading in rice, hides and tobacco.

Ningsia-Hui. 37 0N 106 0E. Autonomous Region. Situated south of Inner Mongolia and covering 25,600 square miles. Population c. 2.5 million. The Hwang Ho River crosses it. The river valley is irrigated and crops of wheat, kaoliang and beans are grown.

Peking. 39 49N 116 30E. Capital of China and its chief political and cultural centre. Contains 2 universities, Peking (founded in 1898) and Tsing-hua (founded in 1912 by Sun Yat-sen). Has an important railway junction and airport, as well as being a major manufacturing centre.

Shanghai. 31 15N 121 35E. Largest city in the world in terms of population (c. 10.8 million). One of the world's principal seaports and an independent municipality, which stands on the Hwang-pu River. Exports raw silk, hog bristles, tea, and tung oil. A mere fishing village in the 11th century, Shanghai became significant after the Treaty of Nanking (1842), when it was opened to foreign trade.

Shenyang. 41 50N 124 0E. Formerly Mukden and chief commercial centre, manufacturing iron and steel and chemicals. An ancient walled city, at various times capital of China from the 3rd century B.C. Visited by Marco Polo in the 13th century.

Sining. 36 40N 100 45E. Capital of Tsinghai Province, on the Sining River. Commercial centre: trades in cereals, wool, salt, timber.

Taipei. Capital of Taiwan. Population (1968) 1,221,112. Commercial centre.

Sinkiang-Uighur. 40 30N 87 0E. Autonomous Region. Situated in the N.W. Population c. 7 million. Rainfall scanty and temperatures extreme. Wheat, maize, cotton and fruits.

Taiwan (Formosa). 24N 121 0E. Island off the coast of S.E. China. Population (1968) 13,297,000. Last stronghold of the Nationalists under Chiang Kai-shek. Predominantly an agricultural economy, whose main food crop is rice and sweet potatoes. Supported economically by the U.S.A.

Taiyuan. 38 2N 112 20E. Industrial centre in a coal-mining district in Shansi Province. Manufactures agricultural and textile machinery. Ancient city, walled in 14th century to protect it against Mongol attacks.

Tibet. 32 30N 88 0E. Autonomous region in the S.W., bordered on the south by India, Bhutan, Sikkim and Nepal and on the west by Kashmir. The most extensive high plateau region in the world, with an average height of 10,000 feet.

Tientsin. 39 0N 117 5E. Capital of Hopei Province and third largest city in China, situated on the Grand Canal and the Hai-ho River. Population c. 4.5 million. Manufactures iron and steel, chemicals and textiles.

Tsinan. 36 45N 117 0E. Capital of Shantung Province. Railway junction and industrial centre, specializing in railway engineering and flour milling.

Urumchi. 44 0N 88 0E. Capital of Sinkiang-Uighur A.R., situated at a height of 9,000 feet. Flour milling and tanning are its main industries.

Wuhan. 30 45N 114 15E. Capital of Hupei Province and largest city in central China. Manufactures textiles and chemicals. Trades in tea, cotton and other agricultural produce.

Yangtse-kiang. 31 45N 121 15E. The longest river in Asia (3,400 miles) and China's chief commercial river. A highway of immense importance, with four of the country's greatest cities—Chungking, Wuhan, Nanking and Shanghai—on or near its banks.

Index

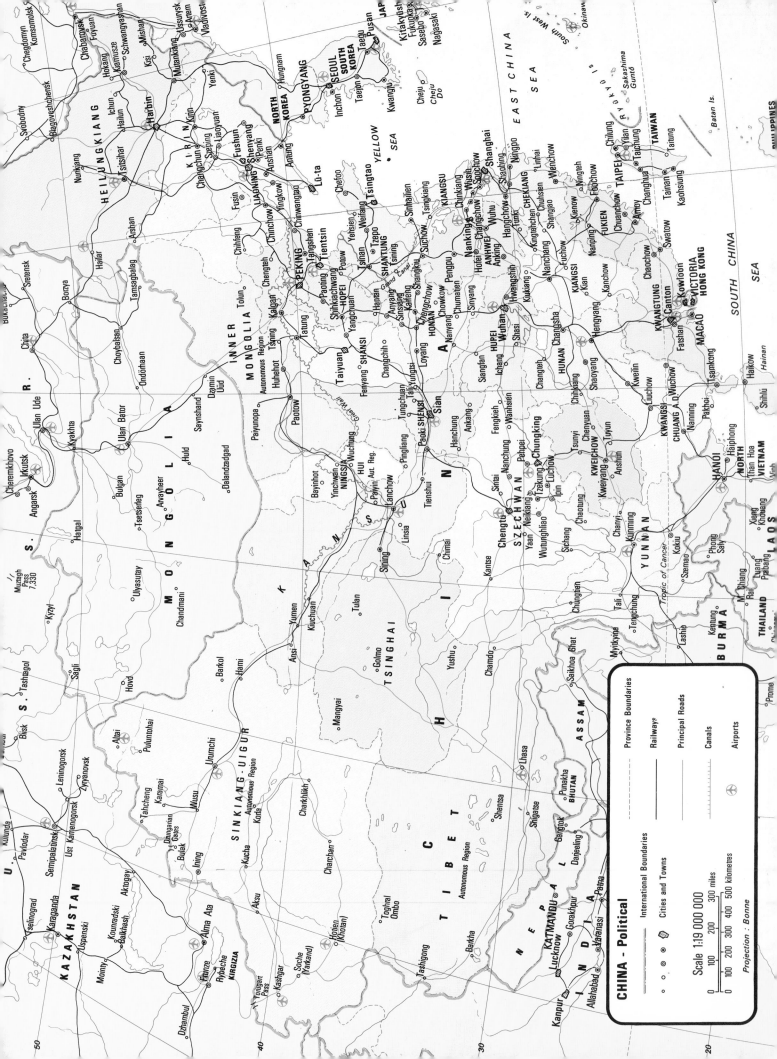

CHINA - Political

	International Boundaries		Province Boundaries
∘ ⊙ ⦿ 🏛	Cities and Towns		Railways
			Principal Roads
			Canals
		✈	Airports

Scale 1:19 000 000

100 0 100 200 300 400 500 kilometres
0   100   200   300 miles

Projection : Bonne

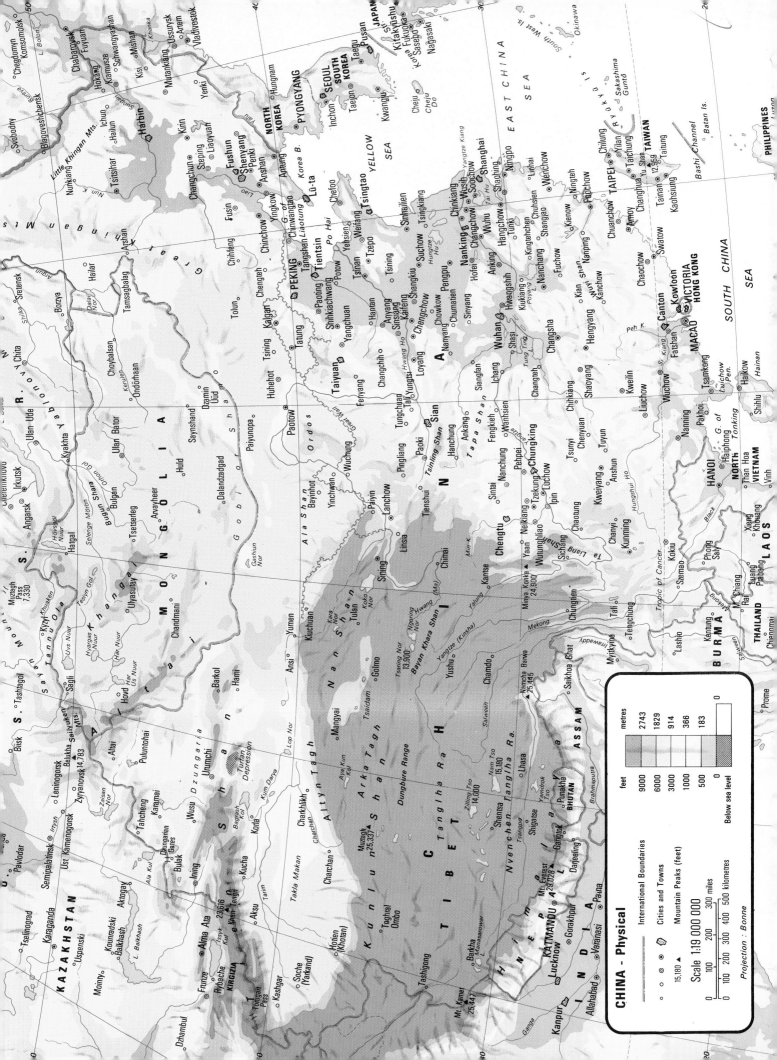

CHINA - Physical

Scale 1:19 000 000

Projection : Bonne

International Boundaries
○ ⊙ ◉ **Cities and Towns**
▲ **Mountain Peaks (feet)**
15,180

feet	metres
9000	2743
6000	1829
3000	914
1000	366
500	183
0	0
Below sea level	

0   100 200 300 miles
0 100 200 300 400 500 kilometres

1 2 3 4 5 6 7 8 9 10-McN-81 80 79 78 77 76